Sustainable Lifestyle Mastery: Transforming Your Life and the Planet

BAILEY HODGSON

Sustainable Lifestyle Mastery

Table of Contents

Sustainable Lifestyle Mastery

Sustainable Lifestyle Mastery

Sustainable Living

Conclusion: A Lifetime of Sustainable Mastery

Appendix: Resources for Sustainable Living

Index

Sustainable Lifestyle Mastery

Introduction: The Call to Sustainable Living

Embracing a Sustainable Mindset

Welcome to the innovative journey of embracing a sustainable mindset, an essential foundation for pursuing a harmonious relationship between humanity and the planet we call home. As a sustainability expert, I am excited to guide you through this in-depth study, inviting you to change perspectives and contribute to a world where conscious choices pave the way for a prosperous future.

Understanding the Urgency:

Unprecedented environmental challenges have made it clear that there is an urgent need to adopt a sustainable mindset. Climate change, resource depletion, and biodiversity loss force us to rethink our lifestyles and recognize the profound impact our choices have on the delicate balance of Earth's ecosystems.

Defining a Sustainable Mindset:

At its core, a sustainable mindset is a conscious effort to balance personal well-being with environmental health. It's about understanding the interconnectedness of our choices and the broader consequences they have. It's about recognizing that every decision we make, from the products we consume to the energy we use, plays a role in shaping the world around us.

The Ripple Effect of Individual Choices:

Think about this: the choices we make in our daily lives send ripples across the world. By embracing a sustainable mindset, you become a catalyst for positive change. Small, intentional actions accumulate to create a significant impact, creating a sense of responsibility for the well-being of our planet and future generations.

Overcoming Barriers to Change:
Adopting a sustainable mindset requires letting go of entrenched habits and social norms that may contribute to environmental degradation. It's about navigating the problems of convenience, consumerism, and a throwaway culture. However, through awareness, education, and determination, these obstacles can be overcome, leading to an intentional and sustainable lifestyle.

Educating for Sustainability:
Education is a powerful ally in stimulating a sustainable mindset. By promoting eco-literacy, we help people make informed decisions that protect the environment. Sustainable education goes beyond textbooks; it promotes a deep understanding of the interconnectedness of humans and

nature and instills a sense of responsibility for the well-being of our planet.

As we embark on this journey together, envision a world where a sustainable mindset is not just a choice, but a way of life. It is a commitment to the delicate dance of coexistence between humanity and Earth, where every decision we make reflects a collective desire for a restorative and thriving future. Embracing a sustainable mindset is not just an individual effort; it's a collective journey into a world where sustainability is woven into the fabric of our thoughts, actions, and aspirations.

The Impact of Individual Choices on the Planet

In the complex web of our lives, every decision we make sends a ripple effect through the delicate balance of Earth's ecosystem. As a sustainability expert, let's delve deeper into the significance of individual choices and how they intricately determine the health and vitality of our planet.

Recognizing the Power of Personal Choices:
It's easy to underestimate the impact of our everyday decisions, from the products we buy to the mode of transportation we choose. However, in the magnificent tapestry of global sustainability, each choice serves as a brushstroke, contributing to the canvas of environmental well-being or degradation. Recognizing the power inherent in these decisions is the first step to creating a conscious and impactful lifestyle.

Consumer Choice and Supply Chain Impact:
Think about your role as a consumer - your choices influence the demand for products and services. By choosing sustainably sourced products, supporting eco-conscious

brands, and reducing waste, we are actively contributing to the shift towards demand-driven environmentally friendly practices within the supply chain. This, in turn, encourages businesses to use more sustainable and ethical production methods.

Energy and Resource Consumption:

From the energy we use to power our homes to the resources embedded in the products we consume, our daily activities have a significant impact on Earth's natural systems. Adopting energy-efficient technologies, reducing water consumption, and embracing circular economy principles become powerful tools to reduce pressure on limited resources.

Transportation and Carbon Footprint:

The mode of transport we choose has far-reaching consequences on the environment. Whether you choose public transportation, carpool, or invest in eco-friendly vehicles, these choices directly contribute to or reduce the carbon footprint associated with daily commutes and travel.

Waste Reduction and Circular Living:

In a throwaway culture, the choices we make about how waste is disposed of matter immensely. By prioritizing recycling, reducing single-use plastics, and adopting a circular approach to consumption where products are designed with end-of-life considerations, we actively participate in minimizing the burden of waste on our ecosystems.

The Butterfly Effect of Collective Consciousness:

When individuals make sustainable choices, they become catalysts for broader change. Collective consciousness, based on deliberate, intentional decisions, has the power to influence societal norms, government policies, and industry practices. What starts as personal choices can become a transformative force for a positive impact on the environment.

In the complex dance between individual decisions and the well-being of the planet, each choice becomes a thread woven into the fabric of our shared future. It is a tapestry crafted by millions of people, each making choices that collectively shape the trajectory of environmental health. As a sustainability expert, I encourage you to think about the profound impact of your daily decisions and recognize the potential for positive change inherent in each decision. Let's embark on a journey of conscious choices that not only demonstrate our commitment to a sustainable present but also create an environmental legacy for future generations.

Chapter 1: Understanding Sustainability

Defining Sustainable Living

As a devoted sustainability specialist, I invite you to explore the deeper concept of sustainable living - a harmonious and intentional way of coexisting with our planet. This chapter serves as a compass, guiding you through the principles and practices that embody the essence of sustainable living.

- **Understanding Sustainability:**

At its core, sustainability goes beyond environmental concerns; it includes a holistic approach that considers social, economic, and ecological dimensions. It is about finding balance, and recognizing that human well-being, prosperity, and the planet are interdependent aspects of a sustainable existence.

The Three Pillars of Sustainability:
Sustainable living is often expressed in three interrelated pillars: environmental responsibility, social equity, and economic viability. These pillars form the basis of a balanced and enduring framework for human life on Earth.

1. **Environmental Responsibility:**
- Embracing practices that minimize harm to ecosystems
- Conserving natural resources and biodiversity
- Reducing pollution and carbon footprint

2. **Social Equity:**
- Ensuring fair treatment and opportunities for all individuals

- Promoting inclusive communities and cultural diversity
- Upholding human rights and social justice.

3. Economic Viability:

- Cultivating a resilient economy that supports local communities
- Promoting ethical business practices and fair trade
- Balancing economic growth with environmental and social considerations

Mindful Consumption:

Sustainable living requires a conscious approach to consumption. It involves making informed choices about the products we use, the food we eat, and the resources we depend on. By prioritizing quality over quantity, choosing eco-friendly alternatives, and embracing a minimalist mindset, people can significantly reduce their impact on the environment.

Energy Efficiency and Renewable Resources:
A cornerstone of sustainable living is the responsible use of energy. This includes adopting energy-efficient technologies, reducing overall energy consumption, and harnessing renewable sources such as solar and wind power. By switching to clean energy sources, we contribute to a more sustainable and resilient energy landscape.

Localism and Community Engagement:
Sustainable living emphasizes the importance of local communities. Supporting local businesses, participating in community initiatives, and fostering a sense of connection with your neighbors are essential components. This not only reduces the ecological footprint associated with global

supply chains but also strengthens the fabric of communal welfare.

Embracing a Circular Economy:
Moving away from the linear "take, make, dispose" model, sustainable living embraces a circular economy. This involves designing products with longevity, prioritizing repair and recycling, and minimizing waste. The goal is to create a closed-loop system that conserves resources and reduces waste through recycling and repurposing.

As we navigate the complex landscape that defines sustainable living, we must envision it as a conscious and transformative journey. It is a commitment to living in harmony with the Earth, where every decision we make reflects an understanding of our interconnectedness and our commitment to leaving a positive impact for future generations. By defining sustainable living, we promote a regenerative relationship with our planet but also encourage a global movement towards a more balanced and sustainable future.

The Three Pillars of Sustainability

As we begin our journey toward understanding sustainable living, it is essential to discover the complex tapestry woven by the three pillars of sustainability. As a dedicated sustainability specialist, I invite you to explore the deep dimensions that form the foundation of a balanced and sustainable approach to our existence on Earth.

1. ***Environmental Responsibility***: A deep commitment to environmental responsibility is at the heart of sustainability. This pillar requires mindful management of our planet's delicate ecosystems. It involves

adopting practices that minimize harm,

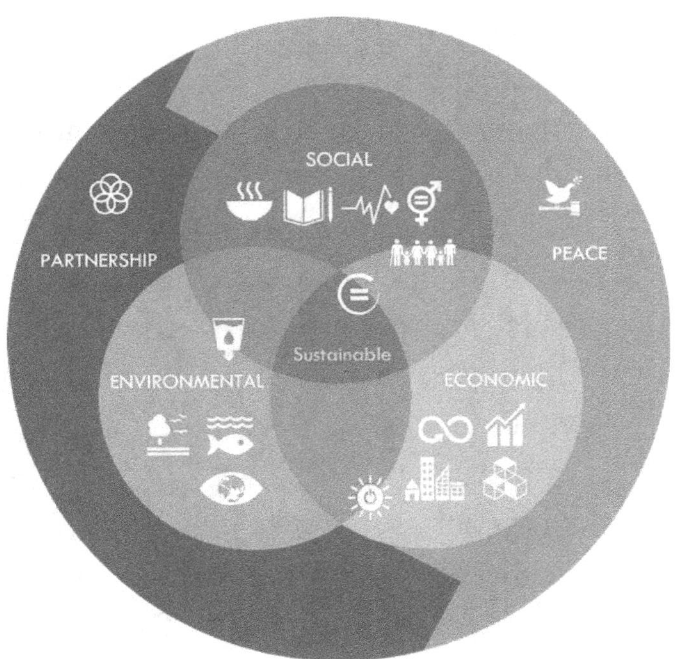

conserve natural resources, and mitigate our impacts on biodiversity. From reducing carbon footprints to protecting endangered species, environmental responsibility compels us to become stewards of our planet, recognizing that the environment's

Sustainable Lifestyle Mastery

health is intricately linked to the well-being of all living things.

2. **Social Equity:** Sustainability is much broader than the ecological realm, reaching into the social fabric of human existence. The pillar of social equity emphasizes the need for fairness, inclusion, and justice for all. It calls for communities that celebrate diversity, uphold human rights, and ensure equal opportunities. By prioritizing social well-being, sustainable living becomes a force for positive change, enabling individuals and communities to thrive in an environment that respects the dignity and rights of every person.

3. **Economic Viability:** From a sustainability perspective, economic viability is not only about profit but also about creating a resilient and balanced economy. This pillar

promotes ethical business practices, fair trade, and the pursuit of a balance between economic growth and environmental and social considerations. Sustainable living seeks to foster economies that support local communities, prioritize responsible production and consumption, and uphold the principles of economic justice.

The Interconnectedness of the Pillars

The brilliance of the three pillars lies in their interconnectedness. A pillar cannot stand alone; each relies on the strength and support of the other. A sustainable future requires a delicate balance between environmental responsibility, social equity, and economic viability. It is a delicate dance in which human well-being, prosperity, and the planet intertwine to create a resilient tapestry that sustains life and promotes harmony.

Living in Harmony with the Three Pillars
Embracing the three pillars of sustainability is not just a theoretical framework but a practical experience. It is a journey of conscious consumption, conscious community engagement, and ethical decision-making. As individuals and communities, we have the power to contribute to the strength of these pillars, paving the way to a future where balance and resilience are the cornerstones of our existence.

In the realm of sustainability, the three pillars serve as beacons of hope, leading us to a world where humanity and the Earth live in harmony. Let us begin this journey of change by recognizing that by upholding the principles of environmental responsibility, social equity, and economic viability, we create the legacy of a prosperous future for generations to come.

Sustainable Lifestyle Mastery

Chapter 2: Eco-Conscious Consumerism

The Power of Informed Choices

In the complex dance between everyday decisions and global impact, the essence of sustainable living emerges from the power of informed choices. As a staunch advocate of sustainable practices, let's explore how every

Susta

decision made, when made with awareness and understanding, becomes a catalyst for positive change - both individually and on a planetary scale.

Understanding the Impact:

To harness the power of informed choices, it is essential to recognize the far-reaching consequences of every decision we make. Whether it's choosing the products we consume, the energy sources we rely on, or the companies we support, every decision helps shape our world. Informed choices lay the foundation for a sustainable lifestyle that aligns with environmental, social, and economic well-being.

Consumer Influence:

One of the most potent realms where we can see the power of informed choice is consumer behavior. By being aware of the environmental and ethical practices of companies, people can actively influence the market. Choosing products that adhere to sustainability principles sends a clear message-consumers demand ethical and eco-friendly alternatives. This ripple effect leads companies to adopt more responsible practices that transform their industries.

Shaping Industries and Supply Chains:
Informed choices wield transformative influence not only at the consumer level but also throughout industries and supply chains. Demand-driven change is encouraged when individuals prioritize products with transparent and sustainable supply chains. This, in turn, encourages businesses to adopt environmentally friendly practices, ethical sourcing, and fair working conditions, fostering a holistic transformation in production methods.

Energy Consumption and Renewable Resources:

In the realm of energy, the power of informed choices is very important. People who know about renewable energy sources can actively choose cleaner alternatives. By choosing renewable energy sources such as solar or wind energy, individuals contribute to reducing their dependence on fossil fuels and contributing to the development of sustainable energy solutions. This informed choice reflects not only personal energy costs but also broader efforts to combat climate change.

Lifestyle Practices:

Sustainable living is woven into the fabric of everyday practices. From transportation options to waste reduction strategies, informed decisions guide people toward eco-friendly alternatives. Carpooling, using public transport, reducing single-use plastics, and adopting circular economy practices are examples of how lifestyle choices, when informed by sustainability principles, become a force for positive change.

Educating for Informed Choices:
Empowering individuals to make informed choices is fundamental to sustainable living. Education and awareness initiatives play a key role in promoting a culture of sustainability. By providing accessible information about the environmental and social impact of different choices, we help people navigate the complexities of our interconnected world and make decisions that align with their values.

In conclusion, the power of informed choices lies at the foundation of sustainable living. When harnessed collectively, they are a transformative force that can shape industries, influence policies, and contribute to the creation of a more resilient and harmonious world. As we navigate the landscape of conscious decision-making, let us embrace the profound impact inherent in each choice, recognizing it as an opportunity to be stewards of positive change in our personal lives and on a global scale.

Navigating Sustainable Brands and Products

In the dynamic landscape of modern consumerism, the conscious consumer has a powerful tool at their disposal: the ability to explore sustainable brands and products. As a dedicated sustainability expert, let's embark on a journey to unravel the intricacies of ethical consumption, realizing how our choices as consumers can be a driving force for positive change in the world.

The Rise of Conscious Consumerism:

Modern times are witnessing a remarkable change in consumer consciousness. More individuals are becoming aware of the significant impact their purchasing decisions can have on the environment, society, and the overall well-being of the planet. Conscious consumerism is not just a trend; it's an innovative movement that seeks to align personal values with the products and brands people support.

Key Indicators of Sustainability:

Exploring a sustainable brand starts with understanding the key indicators of ethical and environmentally responsible practices. Sustainable brands often prioritize transparency, and provide detailed information about their supply chains, production processes, and commitments to fair labor practices. Look for certifications like Fair Trade, USDA Organic, and B Corp, which demonstrate a commitment to social and environmental responsibility.

Ethical Sourcing and Fair Labor Practices:
Sustainability includes not only environmental considerations but also ethical sourcing and fair labor practices. Conscious consumers are more concerned about the treatment of supply chain employees. Sustainable brands prioritize fair wages, safe working conditions, and respect for human rights, ensuring that all products are the result of ethical and socially responsible practices.

Materials and Resource Use:
The materials used to manufacture a product play a critical role in determining its impact on the environment. Sustainable brands carefully select materials that are renewable, recyclable, or biodegradable. Our choice of materials, whether it's organic cotton clothing, reclaimed wood furniture or

minimal environmental impact packaging, reflects our commitment to reducing resource consumption and minimizing waste.

Circular Economy Practices:
What distinguishes sustainable brands is that they adopt the principles of the circular economy. Rather than following the traditional linear model of "take, make, dispose," these brands focus on creating products with longevity in mind. This includes designing for durability, repairability, and recyclability, encouraging consumers to engage in responsible end-of-life practices.

Community Engagement and Social Impact:
Beyond the product itself, conscious consumers also consider the broader impact a brand has on their community. Sustainable brands often participate in community initiatives, support local economies, and contribute to social causes. Understanding a

brand's commitment to social impact can give you a holistic view of its contributions to the well-being of both people and the planet.

Educating yourself as a Consumer:

Empowering yourself as a conscious consumer requires ongoing education. Stay informed about sustainable practices, certifications, and industry standards. Use resources from environmental organizations, ethical fashion guides, and sustainable living platforms to make informed decisions that align with your values.

Making Informed Choices:

As we explore the landscape of sustainable brands and products, let's recognize the transformative potential inherent in every purchase. By making smart choices, conscious consumers not only support social and environmental responsibility but also contribute to market change, inspiring many brands to adopt sustainability as a core aspect of their corporate ethos.

Simply put, exploring sustainable brands and products is a dynamic and evolving process. It involves an honest effort to align purchasing decisions with personal values, ultimately contributing to a more sustainable and just world. As you begin your journey as a conscious consumer, may your choices be guided by a commitment to positive change, one product at a time.

Breaking Free from Consumerism

One of the most innovative steps in the pursuit of sustainable living is breaking free from the shackles of consumerism. As a passionate advocate of environmental well-being, let's embark on a journey to understand the profound implications of consumerism and explore pathways that enable a conscious and sustainable lifestyle.

Understanding the Consumerist Culture:

Consumerism, based on the belief that happiness comes from the endless pursuit and consumption of material goods, has become a common feature of modern society. This promotes a throwaway culture in which products are often designed for obsolescence, contributing to resource depletion, environmental degradation, and an endless cycle of dissatisfaction.

The Environmental Toll of Consumerism:

Consumerism takes a huge toll on the environment. The production, transportation, and disposal of goods contribute to greenhouse gas emissions, deforestation, pollution, and the depletion of natural resources. Breaking free from this cycle becomes not just an individual choice but a shared responsibility for the health of our planet.

Sustainable Lifestyle Mastery

Mindful Consumption as a Counterbalance:
At the core of breaking free from consumerism lies the concept of conscious consumption. This involves making intentional choices about what we purchase, considering the environmental and social impact of the products we buy. Mindful consumers prioritize quality over quantity, longevity over disposability, and sustainable practices over exploitative ones.

Embracing Minimalism:
Minimalism serves as a powerful antidote to consumerism. With a minimalist lifestyle, people intentionally organize their lives and focus on things that add value and purpose. This intentional approach challenges the notion that happiness is synonymous with accumulation, fostering satisfaction with fewer possessions, and a deeper connection to what truly matters.

Sustainable Lifestyle Mastery

The Role of Ethical and Sustainable Brands:
Breaking free from consumerism doesn't mean abstaining from all purchases; rather, it is about making choices that are consistent with ethical and sustainable values. Supporting brands that prioritize transparency, ethical sourcing, and environmental responsibility becomes a conscious act of supporting practices that contribute positively to the world.

Cultivating a Circular Mindset:
The transition to a circular economy is an important aspect of breaking free from consumerism. This involves reviewing the product life cycle, encouraging repairability, recycling, and reuse. By embracing a circular mindset, individuals contribute to reducing waste and minimizing the environmental impact of their consumption.

Investing in Experiences over Possessions:
Consumerism often centers around the acquisition of material possessions. Breaking this vicious cycle involves a shift towards valuing experiences over things. Devoting time and resources to experiences, relationships, and personal growth fosters a sense of fulfillment that transcends the temporary satisfaction of material possessions.

Educating and Inspiring Others:
Breaking free from consumerism is not just a personal journey; it is an opportunity to inspire others. By sharing knowledge, advocating conscious living, and demonstrating the benefits of a sustainable lifestyle, individuals become catalysts for broader social change.

The Liberating Journey towards Sustainability:

Freedom from consumerism is a liberating journey that aligns personal values with actions that benefit the planet and its inhabitants. This is a radical shift from a culture of excess to one of conscious abundance. It's about recognizing the wealth that comes from cultivating a sustainable, balanced, and purpose-driven lifestyle.

In conclusion, breaking free from consumerism is a powerful choice with far-reaching implications. This is a step towards declaring independence from a culture that equates happiness with accumulation and a step that embraces a more harmonious and sustainable way of life. As a sustainability expert, I invite you to embark on this transformational journey and discover the freedom that comes from living consciously and intentionally.

Sustainable Lifestyle Mastery

Chapter 3: Greening Your Home

Energy-Efficient Homes: Tips and Upgrades

As a dedicated sustainability expert, let's explore the enlightening world of energy-efficient homes, an important aspect of our collective efforts to promote a sustainable future. From small changes to transformative upgrades, this journey towards energy efficiency not only reduces your environmental footprint but also provides long-term economic benefits and improves the comfort of your living space.

Understanding the Impact of Home Energy Consumption:

The home, often considered a sanctuary, is also a significant consumer of energy. From lighting and heating to appliances and insulation, various elements contribute to overall energy consumption. Understanding the impact of these components is the first step in making your home an efficient and eco-friendly haven.

Lighting Solutions for Sustainability:
A seamless shift towards energy efficiency starts with your lighting choices. Known for their long life and low energy consumption, LED bulbs are an excellent replacement for traditional incandescent bulbs. Implementing smart lighting and utilizing natural light through well-placed windows further enhances the efficiency and ambiance of living spaces.

Enhancing Heating and Cooling Efficiency:
Heating and cooling systems play an important role in energy consumption.

Regular maintenance, good insulation, and upgrading to energy-efficient HVAC systems can go a long way in reducing energy consumption. Smart thermostats add an intelligent touch by optimizing temperatures according to the layout of the room, ensuring comfort while reducing energy consumption.

Investing in Energy-Efficient Appliances: The appliances we choose have a significant impact on our overall energy consumption. Choosing Energy Star-rated appliances ensures that they meet rigorous efficiency standards. From refrigerators to washing machines, these appliances not only save energy but also contribute to long-term cost savings.

Sealing the Envelope:

Any gaps or leaks that may compromise insulation should be sealed to improve the efficiency of your home. Weatherstripping windows and doors, insulating roofs and walls, and ensuring proper ventilation contribute to a well-sealed envelope. This not only improves energy efficiency but also enhances the overall comfort of living spaces.

Harnessing Solar Power:

The use of renewable energy sources is a transformative step towards sustainability. As technology advances and costs drop, solar panels give homeowners the ability to generate clean energy. In addition to reducing electricity bills, solar power contributes to a decentralized and resilient energy grid.

Water Conservation Practices:
Water-efficient fixtures, such as low-flow toilets and aerated faucets, play an important role in both water conservation and energy efficiency. Reducing hot water usage not only saves water resources but also reduces the energy needed to heat the water. Collecting rainwater for non-potable uses further contributes to a holistic approach to resource management.

Smart Home Integration:
Integrating smart home technologies adds a layer of intelligence to energy management. Smart thermostats, lighting systems, and home automation platforms allow homeowners to monitor and control energy use in real-time. This level of control not only increases efficiency but also empowers

individuals to make informed decisions about their energy use.

Educating and Inspiring Sustainable Living:
As a sustainability professional, it's important not only to implement energy-saving practices but also to inspire others. Providing information on the benefits of energy efficiency, sharing success stories, and providing advice on accessible upgrades contribute to a wider societal shift towards sustainable living.

Long-Term Benefits and Environmental Impact:
The journey to an energy-efficient home is not just about short-term gains. It is an investment for long-term benefits. Reduced energy costs, higher property values, and a diminished environmental footprint are just a few of the many benefits of embracing sustainability in our living spaces.

In conclusion, the pursuit of an energy-efficient home is a brilliant path to sustainable living. It involves a harmonious combination of conscious choices, technological advancements, and efforts to minimize our impact on the planet. As we light up our homes with energy-efficient practices, we simultaneously brighten the prospects of a more sustainable and resilient future.

Minimalist Living for Maximum Impact

In the dynamic landscape of sustainable living, the minimalist philosophy of living emerges as a powerful catalyst for maximum impact. As a sustainability expert, let's explore the transformative realm of minimalism and how simplifying your life not only reduces your impact on the environment but also fosters a deeper sense of purpose and well-being.

Unveiling the Essence of Minimalism:
Minimalism means more than the mere act of decluttering; it's a holistic lifestyle that focuses on conscious choices, mindful consumption, and what truly matters. Fundamentally, minimalist living challenges traditional narratives that equate happiness with material possessions, encouraging people to reevaluate their relationship with possessions and embrace a life of purpose.

Sustainable Consumption through Intentional Choices:
The key to minimalist living is a conscious shift from consumerism to intentional consumption. By living a life that prioritizes quality over quantity, individuals can reduce their ecological footprint. Investing in durable, multi-functional items and choosing experiences over possessions aligns with

principles of sustainability, promoting a flexible and resource-efficient lifestyle.

Environmental Impact of Decluttering:

The act of decluttering isn't just about creating physical space; it also has environmental implications. Responsible disposal of unwanted items by recycling, reusing, or donating reduces waste generation. By adopting a circular mindset in the disposal of items, minimalists actively contribute to reducing landfill waste and promoting sustainable waste management systems.

Energy and Resource Efficiency in Minimalist Spaces:

A minimalist home is inherently designed for efficiency. Streamlining possessions reduces the demand for energy-intensive manufacturing processes. Compact living spaces require less heating, cooling, and lighting, which reduces energy consumption. These efficiencies have a positive impact on the overall demand for resources and environmental preservation beyond the home.

Mindful Material Choices:

Minimalist living encourages people to look critically at the materials they introduce into their lives. Choosing sustainable, ethically sourced, and durable materials aligns with our minimalist principles. From furniture to clothing, every item selected is a conscious choice that reflects a commitment to protecting the environment.

Embracing a Circular Economy:

Minimalist living naturally aligns with the principles of the circular economy, an economic model that prioritizes durability, repairability, and recycling. By prioritizing what lasts and adopting a mindset of responsible disposal, minimalists help create a closed-loop system that uses resources efficiently and reduces waste.

Sustainable Lifestyle Mastery

Mindful Consumerism and Ethical Practices:

Minimalist living involves a shift from mindless consumerism to conscious consumer practices. Individuals become advocates for ethical and sustainable brands, supporting companies that prioritize open supply chains, fair labor practices, and environmental responsibility. This intentional approach to consumerism drives the market towards more sustainable and responsible practices.

The Psychological Benefits of Minimalist Living:

In addition to its environmental impact, minimalist living offers profound psychological benefits. A decluttered and purposeful living space creates peace, reduces stress, and improves mental well-being. Freedom from the burden of excessive possessions allows people to focus on the experiences, relationships, and personal growth that contribute to a fulfilling and meaningful life.

Inspiring Others and Cultivating a Movement:

As a sustainability specialist, my journey to minimalist living is not just a personal choice; it is an opportunity to inspire others. By sharing the principles and benefits of minimalist living, people can promote a broader movement towards conscious consumption, environmental responsibility, and a mindful approach to life.

In conclusion, minimalist living emerges as a powerful tool for maximizing a positive impact both personally and for the planet. Through simplicity, intentional consumption, and focusing on what matters, individuals are encouraging a sustainable, purposeful, and harmonious existence. As we explore the landscape of minimalist living, may our choices resonate with the profound impact they have on the world around us.

Sustainable Home Decor and Design

As a dedicated sustainability expert, let's embark on an exciting exploration of sustainable home furnishings and design, where aesthetic excellence meets environmental mindfulness. From conscious selection of materials to innovative design concepts, this journey towards sustainable living spaces not only enhances the aesthetics of our homes but also contributes to a more resilient and environmentally friendly future.

- **Conscious Material Selection:** The foundation of sustainable home decor and design lies in the careful selection of materials. By choosing eco-friendly, recycled, and responsibly sourced materials, you can ensure that every element of your space complies with the principles of environmental management. From reclaimed wood furniture to organic fiber fabrics, any material you choose becomes a commitment to sustainable living.

- **Upcycling and Repurposing Creativity:** The ethics of sustainability include creativity in repurposing and upcycling existing materials. Designing interior decor elements from reclaimed or repurposed items not only adds uniqueness to your space but also helps reduce waste. Sustainable design encourages innovative and resourceful approaches.

- **Energy-Efficient Lighting and Fixtures:** Lighting plays an important role in terms of aesthetics and energy consumption. A sustainable home design incorporates energy-efficient lighting solutions such as LED lights and fixtures. The thoughtful placement of windows and skylights maximizes natural light and reduces the need for artificial lighting during the day. Smart lighting systems further improve energy efficiency through precise control and automation.

- **Biophilic Design for Well-Being:** Biophilic, nature-inspired design not only enhances the visual appeal of a space but also promotes well-being. A connection to the outdoors is created by incorporating natural elements such as plants, sustainable wood, and natural light. This design philosophy creates a sense of calm, improves air quality, and creates a harmonious living environment.

- **Water-Efficient Fixtures and Appliances:** Sustainability in home design extends to water efficiency. Integrating water-saving devices and appliances reduces water consumption and encourages responsible use. From low-flow faucets to high-performance dishwashers, each addition contributes to a more water-efficient living space.

- **Carbon-Neutral Construction Practices:** For those considering new construction or remodeling, adopting carbon-neutral practices will be an important aspect of sustainable home design. Using low-carbon materials, incorporating energy-efficient insulation, and implementing renewable energy solutions can help reduce your home's carbon footprint throughout its life cycle.

- ***Supporting Local Artisans and Fair Trade Practices:*** Sustainable decor is not just about materials; It's also about supporting ethical and fair business practices. Choosing locally crafted items and products from artisans who prioritize fair working conditions ensures that the beauty of your home is intertwined with social responsibility. These choices contribute to the livelihoods of the community and support the principles of ethical consumption.

- ***Modular and Multifunctional Furniture:*** A sustainable design philosophy embraces versatility and longevity. Modular and multifunctional furniture adapts to changing needs and reduces the need for frequent replacement. Multifunctional pieces not only increase the efficiency of the space but also align with the principles of conscious consumption.

- **Educating Homeowners for Sustainable Living:** As a sustainability professional, this journey includes not only designing sustainable spaces but also educating homeowners. Providing information about sustainable practices, highlighting the benefits of eco-friendly choices, and promoting a mindset about responsible living will contribute to the wider movement towards sustainable housing.

In conclusion, sustainable home decor and design are not just trends; they are a conscious choice to integrate environmental mindfulness into the fabric of our living spaces. From the selection of materials to incorporating innovative design concepts, every decision becomes an opportunity to create a home that balances beauty, functionality, and sustainability. As we explore the realm of sustainable living, may our homes become sanctuaries that reflect our aspirations for a harmonious and environmentally conscious future.

Chapter 4: Mindful Eating for a Healthier Planet

The Benefits of Plant-Based Diets

As a passionate advocate for sustainability, let's explore the deeper realms of plant-based diets, where the choices we make on our plates have a huge impact on our well-being and the health of our planet. From vibrant health benefits to ecological sustainability, adopting a plant-based diet can be a transformative journey to a healthier, more conscious lifestyle.

- **Promoting Personal Health and Well-Being:**

Plant-based diets are a vibrant celebration of nutritious, whole foods that offer numerous health benefits. Abundant in fruits, vegetables, legumes, nuts, and whole grains, these diets are rich in essential vitamins, minerals, fiber, and antioxidants. Scientific studies consistently point to the positive effects of a plant-based diet in reducing the risk of chronic diseases such as heart disease, diabetes, and some cancers.

Optimizing Digestive Health:
Fiber, an important part of a plant-based diet, plays an important role in aiding digestion. Abundant in fruits, vegetables, and whole grains, fibers promote regular bowel movements, maintain a healthy gut

microbiome, and support overall gastrointestinal health. A plant-based diet encourages a variety of fiber sources, which promote a healthy digestive system.

Heart Health and Cholesterol Management:
Plant-based diets have been linked to improved cardiovascular health. By emphasizing heart-healthy foods like fruits, vegetables, nuts, and legumes while reducing saturated and trans fats, individuals who follow a plant-based diet often experience reduced cholesterol levels, lower blood pressure, and a reduced risk of heart disease.

Weight Management and Satiety:
When properly balanced, a plant-based diet promotes effective weight management. The abundance of fiber and water-rich foods helps you feel full, promotes satiety, and reduces the likelihood of overeating. When individuals switch to a plant-based diet, they

often maintain or achieve a healthy weight naturally.

Environmental Sustainability:

Beyond personal health, the benefits of a plant-based diet also have implications for environmental sustainability. Livestock farming is a major cause of greenhouse gas emissions, deforestation, and water pollution. Choosing plant-based options reduces the carbon emissions associated with food production, helps conserve natural resources, and reduces the environmental impact of food choices.

Conserving Water Resources:

Plant-based diets are more water-efficient than diets rich in animal products. Plant-based food production generally requires less water than the water-intensive processes of animal production. Switching to plant-based foods supports the conservation of precious water resources and is consistent with sustainable water management practices.

Biodiversity Conservation:

Plant-based food production generally requires less land than animal production. Choosing a plant-based diet can help prevent deforestation and habitat loss, contributing to biodiversity conservation. By reducing the demand for large-scale livestock farming, individuals are actively participating in ecosystem conservation and the protection of endangered species.

Ethical Considerations and Animal Welfare:

Plant-based diets are consistent with ethical considerations for animal welfare. For many people, choosing plant-based foods reflects a desire to reduce harm to animals and choose compassionate foods. Aligning with these ethical values improves the overall well-being of those who prioritize a more humane and conscious lifestyle.

Sustainable Lifestyle Mastery

Economic Viability and Accessibility:
Plant-based diets can also provide economic benefits and increased access to nutritious foods. Plant-based staples such as beans, lentils, rice, and vegetables are often cheaper than animal products, making plant-based diets a cost-effective choice for individuals and families regardless of economic status.

Culinary Diversity and Creativity:
Embracing a plant-based diet opens up a world of culinary diversity and creativity. With a variety of fruits, vegetables, grains, legumes, and plant-based proteins, individuals can discover different tastes, textures, and international cuisines. Plant-based cooking becomes an adventure, inspiring people to enjoy the delicious possibilities that nature has to offer.

In conclusion, the benefits of plant-based diets go beyond personal health; they empathize with the well-being of the Earth and all its inhabitants. By choosing plant-based foods, individuals begin a journey toward vibrant health, environmental sustainability, and a more ethical and compassionate relationship with the food they eat. As we enjoy the bounty of plant-based living, let our choices reflect our commitment to nourishing ourselves and the planet that sustains us.

Locavore Living: Savoring the Bounty of Local and Seasonal Delights

As a strong advocate for sustainable living, let's take a delicious journey into the heart of locavore living as we make the conscious choice to eat local and seasonal foods. This delectable approach not only excites our taste buds but also promotes environmental sustainability, supports local economies, and deepens our connection to the vibrant tapestry of regional agriculture.

Celebrating Seasonal Abundance:

Locavore living is a celebration of nature's seasonal rhythms, inviting us to experience the peak flavors and nutritional richness of our food. By adapting our diets to the changing seasons, we can enjoy a greater variety of flavors while supporting agricultural practices that prioritize biodiversity and natural growth cycles.

Reduce Carbon Footprints:

One of the key environmental benefits of locavore living is the significant reduction in carbon emissions associated with food transport. By sourcing produce, meat, and dairy products from nearby farms, you minimize the distance your food has to be transported, reduce the environmental impact of long-distance transport, and ensure a more sustainable food supply chain.

Preserving Agricultural Heritage:

Choosing local and seasonal foods is a delicious way to preserve and celebrate an area's agricultural heritage. By supporting local farmers and producers, we contribute to the vitality and resilience of our communities. These conscious decisions help protect traditional farming practices, heirloom varieties, and the local ecosystem that defines the unique character of our culinary landscape.

Enhancing Nutritional Quality:
Locally grown and harvested foods are often very nutritious. The short time between harvest and consumption minimizes nutrient loss, allowing you to enjoy products with peak vitality. This not only improves the taste of the meal but also optimizes the health benefits derived from the vitamins, minerals, and antioxidants found in the fresh, seasonal ingredients.

Cultivating Seasonal Connection:
Locavore living fosters a deeper connection with the changing seasons and natural cycles

of the environment. Participating in local farmers markets, Community Supported Agriculture (CSA) programs, and seasonal food festivals becomes an enriching experience that connects us to the ebb and flow of nature's abundance and provides a real connection to the origins of our meals.

Supporting Local Economies:
Choosing locally grown food is a powerful way to strengthen local economies. By investing in local farmers, growers, and food artisans, we contribute to the economic resilience of our communities. This support goes beyond individual transactions to support livelihoods and create strong local food ecosystems.

Diversity on the Plate:
Locavore living encourages us to embrace culinary diversity while exploring the varied tastes that local agriculture has to offer. From heirloom tomatoes grown in the

summer to root vegetables in the fall, each season brings its unique flavor. This variety not only enlivens our meals but also encourages creativity in the kitchen as we adapt to the ever-changing abundance.

Promoting Sustainable Agriculture:
Choosing local and seasonal foods aligns with sustainable farming practices. Many local farmers prefer environmentally friendly farming methods, such as organic or regenerative farming. By supporting these practices, locavore living becomes a catalyst for promoting more sustainable and resilient agricultural systems.

Culinary Adventure and Appreciation:
Locavore living is a culinary adventure that invites us to appreciate and explore the richness of our local terroir. Discovering new tastes, rediscovering forgotten traditional varieties, and savoring the nuances of local cuisine become integral parts of the locavore

experience. This culinary appreciation adds a layer of joy to the act of nourishing ourselves.

In short, locavore living is a wonderful and important choice that extends beyond the boundaries of our plates. It's a commitment to enjoying the interconnectedness of food, community, and environment. As we embrace the abundance of local and seasonal delicacies, may our meals be a vibrant expression of sustainability, culinary exploration, and a deep appreciation for the nutrients our planet so graciously provides.

Reducing Food Waste in Your Kitchen

As a staunch advocate of sustainable living, let's discover techniques to reduce food waste in the kitchen, a culinary journey that not only conserves resources but also changes our approach to nourishment. From conscious meal planning to creative kitchen remodeling: each conscious step contributes to a sustainable and harmonious relationship with the food we bring home.

- ***Mindful Meal Planning:*** The key to reducing food waste is careful meal planning. By thoughtfully considering our weekly meals, we can create a shopping list tailored to our specific needs. This thoughtful approach reduces the likelihood of impulse purchases and ensures efficient use of ingredients, reducing the likelihood of unused items languishing deep in refrigerators.

- ***Embracing Imperfect Produce:*** The journey toward reducing food waste embraces the beauty of imperfect produce. Slightly misshapen fruits or slightly bruised vegetables may not meet standard aesthetic standards, but they are nutritious and flavorful. Supporting initiatives that save "imperfect" products not only reduces waste but also contributes to a more inclusive and sustainable food system.

- ***Clever Storage and Organization:*** Proper storage and organization play an important role in preserving the freshness of our food. Understanding different fruits and vegetables and their optimal storage conditions can help you extend their shelf life. Investing in high-quality storage containers, using air-tight seals, and effectively organizing your kitchen can significantly reduce clutter and unnecessary waste.

- ***Repurposing Leftovers Creatively:*** Transforming leftovers into enticing new dishes is a culinary adventure that reduces food waste. Getting creative in the kitchen can turn last night's roasted vegetables into a delicious frittata or a delicious stir-fry with leftover grains. The most important thing is not to view leftovers as remnants but as ingredients for a fresh and innovative culinary creation.

- **Composting for Nutrient-Rich Soil:** For inevitable food scraps and peelings, composting offers a sustainable solution. Building a composting system in our homes turns organic waste into nutrient-rich soil and closes the loop on the natural food cycle. Composting not only reduces landfill contributions but also provides a valuable resource for nurturing our garden.

- **Understanding Food Expiry Dates:** It takes a keen eye to navigate the maze of food expiration dates. Understanding the differences between "sell by," "use by," and "best before" labels can help you prevent premature discarding of perfectly edible items. Relying on our senses - smell, taste, and sight - becomes an essential part of measuring the freshness and edibility of foods beyond the printed date.

- ***Optimizing Portion Control:*** Optimizing portion control is a powerful strategy for reducing food waste. Being mindful of portion sizes, especially when cooking for smaller households, helps prevent excess food from going uneaten. The goal is to enjoy every meal without generating unnecessary leftovers, which ultimately leads to waste.

- ***Smart Freeze Technology:*** Freezing is a valuable ally in the fight against food waste. Whether you're portioning meals before freezing or preserving seasonal produce at its peak, smart freezing techniques let you enjoy a variety of foods all year round. A well-organized freezer offers a treasure trove of convenience without compromising on durability.

- **Community Sharing Initiatives**: Extending the spirit of reducing food waste to our local community creates a ripple effect of positive impact. By participating in local food-sharing initiatives or contributing to community refrigerators, we can share surplus food with those who could benefit. This joint effort not only reduces waste but also fosters a sense of connection and solidarity.

- **Educating and Advocating for Change**: As sustainability experts in our kitchens, we become catalysts for change by educating others. Sharing tips, recipes, and the importance of reducing food waste with friends, family, and community amplifies the impact of our efforts. Supporting systemic changes in production, distribution, and waste management contributes to a more sustainable and equitable food system.

In conclusion, reducing food waste in our kitchens is a multi-faceted journey that connects culinary creativity with environmental stewardship. Through conscious meal planning, repurposing leftovers, and fostering a deeper appreciation for the resources on our plates, we not only reduce waste but also contribute to a more sustainable and resilient food system. As we indulge in the joys of conscious culinary choices, may our kitchens become vibrant hubs of sustainability where we value every ingredient, enjoy every meal, and reduce our impact on the planet.

Chapter 5: Sustainable Fashion: Dressing with a Conscience

The Environmental Impact of Fast Fashion

As a dedicated advocate of sustainable practices, let's explore the tangled web of fast fashion—a complex tapestry that not only shapes our wardrobes but also has a huge impact on the environment. From resource depletion to textile waste, the journey into the environmental impact of fast fashion highlights the need for a paradigm shift in how we approach clothing consumption.

Rapid Resource Depletion: The frenetic pace of fast fashion demands an insatiable appetite for resources. From water-intensive cotton cultivation to energy-intensive manufacturing processes, the industry puts enormous pressure on scarce resources. Rapid deforestation for textile production and the excessive use of water, chemicals, and energy contribute to environmental degradation, ecosystem disruption, and accelerating climate change.

Textile Pollution: Synthetic fibers such as polyester and nylon, which are synonymous with fast fashion, carry significant environmental costs. These materials shed microfibers when washed, bringing plastic particles into waterways. The accumulation of microplastics poses threats to aquatic life and ecosystems, further exacerbating the planet's pollution crisis.

Chemical Intensive Production: The production of fast fashion clothing relies heavily on the use of chemicals, from pesticides in cotton cultivation to dyes and finishes in textile manufacturing. When these chemicals are discharged into water sources, they not only pollute the ecosystem but also threaten the health of settlements near the production facilities. Toxic runoff from dyeing processes contributes to water pollution, affecting aquatic life and threatening the livelihoods of people who rely on clean water sources.

Throwaway Culture: Fast fashion encourages a throwaway culture where clothes are treated as disposable items rather than lasting investments. Due to rapidly changing trends, consumers tend to throw away clothes after just a few wears, leading to a massive accumulation of textile waste. Landfills are filled with remnants of yesterday's fashion, causing environmental degradation and posing long-term waste management problems.

Human Rights and Labor Exploitation: In addition to environmental issues, the fast fashion industry also deals with issues related to human rights and labor exploitation. Low-cost, high-speed production often leads to poor working conditions, insufficient wages, and a lack of job security for garment workers. The desire to achieve rapid turnover and low production costs can lead to a race to the bottom that threatens the well-being of individuals in the supply chain.

Carbon Footprint and Global Transportation: The globalized nature of fast fashion increases its carbon footprint. The transcontinental transport of raw materials, textiles, and finished products contributes significantly to greenhouse gas emissions. From manufacturing centers to retail locations, every step of the supply chain relies on fossil fuels for transportation, increasing the industry's impact on climate change.

Overconsumption and Fashion Waste: The fast fashion model thrives on overconsumption and the purchase of clothing items at an unprecedented rate. The never-ending cycle of buying, throwing away, and replenishing creates mountains of fashion waste. Landfills are full of clothes that take decades, or even centuries, to decompose, perpetuating the environmental consequences of a hyper-consumerist culture.

The Urgency of Sustainable Alternatives: Given these environmental concerns, the need for sustainable alternatives is becoming increasingly urgent in the fashion industry. Embracing slow fashion, promoting ethical and transparent supply chains, and supporting circular fashion systems that prioritize recycling and upcycling are important steps in reducing the environmental impact of our clothing choices.

In conclusion, the environmental impact of fast fashion prompts us to rethink the threads that weave our wardrobe. As sustainability experts, we recognize the need to move towards responsible consumption and support brands that prioritize environmental responsibility and ethical practices. By discovering the complexities of fast fashion and embracing sustainable alternatives, we contribute to a harmonious relationship between fashion and the environment, ensuring that our choices are aligned with the well-being of the planet and its inhabitants.

Building a Capsule Wardrobe

As a staunch advocate of sustainable living, let's take a look at the art of building a capsule wardrobe - a thoughtful and conscious approach to fashion that transcends trends and finds a harmonious relationship between style and sustainability. From conscious curation to eclectic styling, the capsule wardrobe journey is guided by the principles of longevity, versatility, and environmental responsibility.

- **Defining a Capsule Wardrobe:** A capsule wardrobe is more than just a collection of clothes; it is a carefully curated selection of timeless, high-quality pieces that seamlessly complement one another. Defined by its simplicity and versatility, a capsule wardrobe encourages careful consideration of the value of each garment, ensuring that each piece serves a purpose and stands the test of time.

- **Mindful Curation:** Building a capsule wardrobe begins with careful consideration and a commitment to mindful curation. Instead of following trends, individuals carefully select pieces that suit their style, lifestyle, and the versatility they need for different situations. This deliberate approach reduces impulse purchases and creates a deeper connection with the clothes we choose to adorn ourselves with.

- **Quality over Quantity:** When it comes to capsule wardrobes, quality comes before quantity. Investing in well-made, durable pieces not only ensures longevity but also contributes to a sustainable fashion ecosystem. Choosing clothes made from eco-friendly materials and supporting ethical and transparent brands aligns with the values of environmental responsibility and conscious consumerism.

- **Versatile Styling:** Versatility is the basis of a capsule wardrobe. Each piece is not selected in isolation but rather with an understanding of how it complements other items within the collection. This strategic approach allows for countless outfit combinations and maximizes the potential of each outfit. A well-designed capsule wardrobe transcends the limitations of individual pieces and allows individuals to express their style with creativity and flair.

- **Embracing Timeless Classics:** Timeless classics form the basis of a capsule wardrobe. Essentials like a white shirt, a versatile blazer, and a pair of quality denim jeans serve as enduring foundations. These timeless pieces transition seamlessly between seasons and trends, keeping your wardrobe relevant and stylish over time.

- **Seasonal Edit and Rotation:** Capsule wardrobes are seasonally processed to adapt to changing weather and lifestyle requirements. This intentional rotation involves careful storage of out-of-season items and introducing weather-appropriate pieces. This practice not only preserves streamlined collections but also allows individuals to continually modify their wardrobes according to their evolving styles and needs.

- **Minimalism and Decluttering:** The ethos of minimalism permeates a capsule wardrobe, encouraging people to declutter and simplify their clothing collections. The process of decluttering involves parting ways with items that no longer fit your style or lifestyle, creating space for a careful and curated selection of garments.

- **Environmental Impact:** Building a capsule wardrobe helps reduce environmental impact. By focusing on longevity and conscious consumption, individuals are reducing their demand for fast fashion, which is often associated with resource-intensive production and textile waste. A consciously curated capsule wardrobe adheres to the principles of sustainability and encourages an eco-friendly and more responsible approach to personal style.

- **Personal Expression and Confidence:** Contrary to the notion that a limited closet stifles creativity, a capsule wardrobe becomes a canvas for personal expression. Choosing pieces intentionally allows people to explore their style preferences and experiment with different combinations. This goal-oriented approach fosters a sense of confidence and empowerment, as individuals become architects of their own unique and sustainable style.

In conclusion, building a capsule wardrobe transcends the world of fashion. It is a lifestyle choice that combines style and sustainability. As sustainability experts, we recognize the transformative power of conscious curation, timeless classics, and eclectic style. By embracing the principles of the capsule wardrobe, we're on track to create a legacy of sustainable style that reflects our values, minimizes our environmental impact, and celebrates the timeless beauty of purpose-driven fashion.

Thrifting and Upcycling

Let's unravel the threads of thrifting and upcycling in the realm of sustainable living, a dynamic duo that not only modernizes fashion but also champions ecological responsibility. From the thrill of vintage discoveries to the creative transformations of second-hand, the journey through thrifting and upcycling is a celebration of conscious consumerism and the redefinition of fashion's life cycle.

Thrifting: Thrifting is more than just finding items at bargain prices. It's a purposeful exploration of pre-loved fashion. When people visit thrift stores, vintage stores, or online secondhand platforms, they embark on a treasure hunt where each discovery has its unique history. Not only does thrifting offer a variety of styles, but it also extends the lifecycle of clothing by diverting items from landfills and reducing the demand for new production.

The Joy of Vintage Discoveries: One of the delights of thrifting is the joy of finding vintage gems. From timeless clothing with intricate details to iconic pieces from the bygone era, thrift stores are a haven for those looking to add character and individuality to their wardrobe. Each vintage find tells a story, connecting the past and present and offering a sustainable alternative to fast fashion trends.

Embracing Secondhand Style: Thrifting is a celebration of secondhand style- a conscious choice to adorn oneself with clothes that have a pre-existing narrative. By adopting second-hand fashion, individuals reduce textile waste and the environmental impact associated with producing new clothing. Thrifting aligns with the principles of circular fashion, promoting a cyclical and sustainable approach to the lifecycle of garments.

Upcycling: Complementing thrifting is the art of upcycling - a creative process that transforms old or discarded clothes into fresh and unique pieces. Upcycling challenges the notion of disposability and encourages individuals to reimagine and repurpose existing items. Whether it's turning old denim into a stylish tote bag or transforming vintage fabrics into modern clothing, upcycling breathes new life into fabrics that might otherwise end up in landfills.

The Creative Alchemy of Upcycling: Upcycling is a form of creative alchemy where discarded items are transformed. With a touch of imagination and skill, people can bring their wardrobe to life and personalize it. Upcycled pieces not only showcase your personality but also have environmental benefits by reducing resource consumption and waste generation. This practical approach to fashion aligns with the ethos of sustainability, encouraging individuals to actively participate in the circular economy.

Education and Empowering: Thrifting and upcycling are more than practices, they are educational and empowering movements. Participating in second-hand fashion and upcycling projects can help you gain a deeper understanding of the environmental impact of clothing consumption. It empowers people to make informed choices, challenges disposable cultural norms and encourages a more conscious and sustainable approach to personal style.

Community and Local Economies: Participating in thrifting and upcycling initiatives contributes to the vitality of local communities and economies. Thrift stores, consignment shops, and local artisans working on upcycling projects become integral parts of the sustainable fashion ecosystem. Supporting these businesses not only reduces the carbon footprint associated with global supply chains but also improves community resilience and connection.

Fashion Revolution: Engaging with thrifting and upcycling propels individuals from passive consumers into conscious supporters of the fashion revolution. By choosing second-hand fashion and embracing upcycling, individuals are playing an active role in changing the narrative of the fashion industry. This movement towards a sustainable and circular fashion system challenges the status quo and paves the way for a future where creativity, individuality, and environmental responsibility coexist harmoniously.

In conclusion, the Odyssey through thrifting and upcycling is a journey of conscious choices and creative change. As sustainability experts, we recognize the power of second-hand style and the transformative potential of recycling. By embracing these practices, we contribute to a fashion environment that values the stories behind each garment, minimizes environmental impact, and celebrates the timeless beauty of sustainable style. Thrifting and upcycling are more than just actions, they are essential components of a sustainable style philosophy that encourages us to see fashion as a canvas for creativity, a source of empowerment, and a catalyst for positive change.

Chapter 6: Sustainable Transportation

Eco-Friendly Commuting Options

In the pursuit of sustainable living, let's embark on a journey through eco-friendly travel options- an exploration of transportation options that align with environmental stewardship, reduce carbon emissions, and contribute to the creation of more sustainable urban landscapes. From pedal-powered commutes to electric alternatives, the range of eco-friendly transportation options is diverse and impactful.

- **Pedal Power:** At the forefront of eco-friendly commuting options is the timeless art of cycling. Rediscovering the joy of pedaling transport will not only improve your physical well-being but also significantly reduce carbon emissions. Whether it's commuting to work, running errands, or just enjoying a ride, cycling transforms the daily commute into a sustainable and health-promoting experience.

- **Embracing Public Transport:** Public transport stands as a cornerstone for eco-friendly commuting, offering an efficient means of reducing individual carbon footprints. Buses, trains, trams, and subways offer a shared and energy-efficient alternative to private car travel. By using public transport, people contribute to reducing traffic congestion, improving air quality, and optimizing urban infrastructure.

- **Walking:** The simple act of walking is one of the most sustainable commuting options. Whether you are exploring city streets or navigating sub-urban neighborhoods, walking can reduce your environmental impact while improving your well-being. Walking short distances not only reduces carbon emissions but also connects individuals more closely to their environment.

- **Electric Vehicles:** As technology advances, electric vehicles (EVs) have emerged as a revolutionary solution in the realm of eco-friendly commuting.

Whether it's a car, bicycle, or scooter, EVs use clean energy sources, reducing dependence on fossil fuels. Embracing electric alternatives contributes to a reduction in air pollution and positions individuals as early adopters in the transition to a sustainable transportation future.

- ***Carpooling and Ridesharing:*** Carpooling and ridesharing initiatives leverage the sharing economy to maximize transportation efficiency. By pooling resources and sharing rides, individuals reduce the number of cars on the road, reduce congestion, and lower carbon emissions per passenger. These joint efforts align with the principles of sustainability and highlight the collective impact of shared transportation.

- ***Telecommuting and Remote Work:*** In the digital age, telecommuting, and remote work emerge as powerful tools in the quest for sustainable commuting. Digital connectivity allows individuals to completely reduce the need for daily commutes and embrace flexible work routines that prioritize productivity while reducing environmental impact. Remote work represents a paradigm shift in the way we conceptualize and approach everyday professional routines.

- ***Micro-mobility Solutions:*** Micro-mobility solutions such as electric scooters and bicycles, offer agile and eco-friendly options for short-distance commuting. Accessible through app-based platforms, these micro-mobility alternatives provide convenient, low-emission transportation and further diversify green travel options in urban environments.

- **Urban Planning and Infrastructure Development:** Promoting eco-friendly commuting options goes beyond personal choices to include urban planning and infrastructure development. Building bike lanes, pedestrian-friendly zones, and integrating green spaces into the urban landscape promotes a symbiotic relationship between sustainable transport and urban planning. By prioritizing eco-friendly infrastructure, communities can encourage and promote greener travel practices.

- **Educational Initiatives and Advocacy:** Education initiatives and advocacy play key roles in enabling people to choose sustainable transport. By raising awareness about the environmental impact of commuting habits and promoting the benefits of eco-friendly alternatives, communities can be inspired to make a collective transition to more sustainable modes of transport.

In conclusion, the landscape of eco-friendly commuting options encourages individuals to reimagine their daily journeys with a focus on sustainability. As sustainability experts, we recognize the transformative potential of transportation options that prioritize environmental well-being. By embracing eco-friendly alternatives such as cycling, public transportation, and electric vehicles, we collectively pave the way for greener commutes such as pedaling-shared rides or electric charge at a time. Not only do we reduce carbon emissions by following sustainable transport routes, but also help contribute to the creation of urban environments that prioritize the health of both individuals and the planet.

The Rise of Electric Vehicles

The culmination of change in the symphony of sustainable transportation is the rise of electric vehicles (EVs). As a sustainability specialist, let's take a look at the transformation journey of electric vehicles – a technological revolution that will not only reshape the automotive landscape but also lead us to a greener and more sustainable future.

Emission-Free Innovation: The basis of the development of electric vehicles is the pursuit of emission-free transportation. Unlike conventional combustion engines that rely on fossil fuels, electric vehicles use electricity as their primary energy source. This fundamental change in propulsion technology significantly reduces greenhouse gas emissions and represents a decisive step in the fight against climate change and air pollution.

Advancements in Battery Technology: Essential to the success of electric vehicles is the relentless pursuit of advancements in battery technology. Lithium-ion batteries, due to their high energy density and efficiency, have become a major force behind electric vehicles. Continuous research and innovation in battery technology aims to enhance range, reduce charging times, and improve overall durability, fostering a continuous evolution in the realm of electric mobility.

Accessible Charging Infrastructure: As electric vehicles grow in popularity, so does the development of a robust charging infrastructure. From public charging stations to home solutions, charging stations are becoming more accessible. Expanding this infrastructure is important to eliminate "range anxiety" and make electric vehicles a practical and convenient choice for everyday commuting and long-distance travel.

Diverse Models and Market Adoption: The growth of electric vehicles is moving beyond niche markets, with automakers incorporating sustainable practices into their fleets. From compact city cars to luxury SUVs, more and more car models offer electric variants. This diversification not only increases consumer choice but also positions electric vehicles as a viable option for a wider range of drivers.

Government Incentives and Policy Support: Governments around the world are playing an important role in promoting the growth of electric vehicles through various incentives and policy support. Tax credits, rebates, and subsidies encourage consumers to adopt electric mobility, while regulations encourage automakers to invest in clean technologies. These strategic interventions contribute to an environment where sustainable transportation is economically and environmentally viable.

Economic and Environmental Benefits: The advent of electric vehicles brings many economic and environmental benefits. In addition to reducing carbon emissions, switching to electric vehicles helps reduce air pollution, improve public health, and reduce dependence on fossil fuels. In addition, the growth of the electric vehicle market will generate employment and economic growth in the sustainable mobility sector.

Challenges and Solutions: The advent of electric vehicles has certainly brought about changes, but challenges remain. Overcoming concerns about the environmental impact of charging infrastructure, battery disposal, and manufacturing is critical to ensuring the long-term sustainability of electric vehicles. Continuous research and collaborative efforts between government, industry, and environmentalists are essential to addressing these challenges and improving the trajectory of electric mobility.

Consumer Awareness and Education: As electric vehicles gain momentum, consumer awareness and education will play a critical role in making informed choices. Dispelling myths, addressing concerns, and highlighting the economic and environmental benefits of electric mobility can help people embrace the transition to sustainable transport.

In conclusion, the rise of electric vehicles is an important step towards a greener and more sustainable future. As a sustainability specialist, witnessing this evolution is like observing a transformative force that

Sustainable Lifestyle Mastery

transcends the automotive industry. With electric vehicles, we are moving towards a horizon where transport is fully compatible with environmental protection - a future where the hum of electric motors echoes commitments for cleaner air, lower carbon emissions, and a planet that thrives alongside sustainable mobility.

Sustainable Travel Practices

Embarking on a journey goes beyond the thrill of exploration. It is an opportunity to weave sustainability into the very fabric of our journey. As a sustainability specialist, let's delve deeper into the realm of sustainable travel practices - a conscious approach that honors the planet, respects local communities, and changes the way the world is perceived.

- **Mindful Transportation Choices:** Sustainable travel starts with conscious transportation choices. By choosing environmentally friendly modes of transport such as trains, buses, and electric vehicles, you reduce the impact of your journey on the environment. Embracing slow travel, which has become an essential part of our travel adventures, not only reduces the impact on the environment but also fosters a deeper connection with the landscapes we traverse.

- **Cultural Respect and Local Engagement:** Respecting and interacting with local culture is fundamental to sustainable travel. Sustainable travelers seek to understand and appreciate the traditions, language, and values of the communities they visit, rather than imposing their customs. By supporting local artisans, businesses, and cultural initiatives, travelers actively contribute to the preservation of various global heritages.

- **Eco-Friendly Accommodations:** Choosing eco-friendly accommodation is fundamental to sustainable travel practice. From eco-lodges to eco-certified hotels, conscientious travelers seek accommodations that strive to minimize their impact on the environment. Practices such as energy conservation, waste reduction, and water conservation are essential to building an environmentally friendly hospitality industry.

- **Ethical Wildlife Tourism:** Ethical wildlife tourism is very important to people who are drawn to encounters with wildlife. Responsible travelers choose experiences that prioritize animal welfare and conservation. Nature reserves, rehabilitation centers, and guided tours by conservation experts allow you to enjoy the wonders of nature while protecting endangered species.

- **Plastic-Free Exploration:** Sustainable travelers carry the ethos of "leave no trace" into their explorations. Reducing single-use plastic is a key practice, with reusable water bottles, eco-friendly toiletries, and cloth bags being essential companions. This conscious effort ensures that our footprints on the landscapes we traverse are fleeting and gentle.

- **Community-Led Initiatives:** Supporting community-led initiatives is a powerful way to promote sustainable travel. Whether participating in local tours, workshops, or community projects, travelers actively contribute to the well-being of their destination. This collaborative approach strengthens local economies and ensures that tourism benefits local communities rather than exploiting them.

- **Carbon Offsetting and Responsible Tourism:** Sustainable adventurers are aware of the carbon footprint of their travel and often take steps to offset it. Contributing to projects that promote reforestation, renewable energy, or community development can help reduce the environmental impact of journeys. Responsible tourism, based on ethical decision-making, ensures that our travels enrich, rather than harm, the places we value.

- **Educational and Mindful Experiences:** Sustainable travel is an opportunity for continuous learning and meaningful experiences. Your understanding deepens as you interact with local guides, participate in eco-tours, and immerse yourself in the history and ecology of your destination. This educational aspect of travel becomes a platform to raise global awareness and encourage responsible citizenship.

- **Promoting Conservation through Adventure:** Sustainable travel is not only about preserving the environment but also actively contributing to conservation efforts. Adventure activities that promote conservation, such as eco-trekking, sustainable diving, and wildlife viewing, offer exciting experiences while encouraging a sense of responsibility for preserving our planet's natural wonders.

In conclusion, sustainable travel practices weave a symphony of responsible choices, cultural respect, and environmental stewardship. As a sustainability professional, witnessing the global shift toward conscious exploration is like seeing the world as a sanctuary entrusted to us to protect and nurture. Through sustainable travel, we become stewards of the Earth, nurturing it for future generations and ensuring that the wonders we encounter are preserved for years to come.

Chapter 7: Zero Waste Living

The Principles of Zero Waste

In the realm of sustainable living, the zero waste principle has emerged as a leading star, paving the way to a world where resourcefulness triumphs over waste. As a sustainability expert, let's explore the core principles of zero waste and discover a philosophy that will transform the way we consume, dispose of, and live in harmony with our planet.

1. **Reduce Consumption:** At the heart of zero waste is a radical change in our approach to consumption. Accepting the principle of reducing consumption challenges the notion of disposable culture. By carefully evaluating our needs, making informed purchasing decisions, and investing in high-quality, long-lasting goods, we become architects of a lifestyle that prioritizes longevity over disposability.

2. **Refusing Single-Use Plastics:** One of the cornerstones of a zero-waste lifestyle is the refusal to use single-use plastics. This commitment goes beyond reusable bags and water bottles to include a complete rejection of single-use packaging. By choosing unpackaged or bulk items and supporting companies that support plastic-free alternatives, Zero Wasters is actively helping to reduce plastic pollution.

3. **Reusing and Repairing:** The principles of reuse and repair emphasize techniques that extend the lifecycle of items. Zero wasters embrace the challenge of repairing, repurposing, and creatively reinventing items to prevent them from reaching landfills prematurely. This ethos not only fosters a culture of creativity but also

fosters a deep appreciation for the stories behind beloved possessions.

4. **Recycling with Intention:** Recycling is an important aspect of waste management, but Zero Wasters takes a conscious approach to it. The principles of recycling with intention involve understanding local recycling systems, prioritizing readily recyclable materials, and supporting systematic improvements. Zero waste enthusiasts see recycling as a last resort and emphasize the importance of reducing and reusing things before resorting to the recycling bin.

5. **Composting:** Composting is a natural ally in the zero waste process. Zero Wasters actively participates in closing the loop in the circular economy by diverting organic waste from landfills and turning it into nutrient-rich

compost. Composting not only reduces methane emissions but also nourishes the soil, creating a regenerative cycle that aligns with nature's principles.

6. **Mindful Consumerism:** A zero-waste lifestyle promotes conscious consumerism - a practice based on supporting businesses and products that align with sustainability values. By selecting products with minimal packaging, prioritizing ethically sourced materials, and supporting companies committed to environmental responsibility, zero wasters wield their purchasing power to drive positive change in the marketplace.

7. **Community Engagement:** Zero waste principles go beyond individual action and include community engagement. Getting involved in local initiatives,

sharing knowledge, and collaborating with neighbors and businesses will amplify the impact of your zero-waste practices. Through collaborative efforts, zero wasters contribute to the creation of resilient and environmentally conscious communities.

8. **Continuous Learning:** The concept of continuous learning is at the heart of the zero waste principle. Zero wasters recognize that the journey towards a waste-free lifestyle is an evolving process. By keeping abreast of sustainable practices, being open to new ideas, and adapting to new solutions, we ensure zero waste advocates are at the forefront of positive environmental change.

In conclusion, the principles of zero waste orchestrate a dance in harmony with the

Earth. That is, a dance where every step is conscious and every choice resonates with environmental awareness. As a sustainability professional, witnessing the adoption of zero waste principles is like witnessing a collective awakening. It is our shared commitment to reorganize waste into resources and support a world where zero waste principles lead to a more sustainable and resilient future.

Tips for Reducing Household Waste

Transforming our homes into havens of sustainability starts with conscious choices and intentional actions. As a sustainability specialist, let's take a look at a variety of practical tips for reducing household waste-a journey that not only benefits the environment but also transform our homes into beacons of conscious living.

- **Embrace a Zero-Waste Lifestyle:** Consider adopting a zero-waste lifestyle as your guiding philosophy. It entails a holistic approach to waste reduction, emphasizing the principles of refuse, reduce, reuse, recycle and rot. By aligning daily habits with these principles, households can significantly reduce their carbon footprint.

- **Conduct a Waste Audit:** Embark on a waste audit adventure to understand the composition of household waste. By sorting and weighing discarded items over time, households gain insight into the areas where waste reduction efforts will have the greatest impact. This knowledge serves as a compass for initiatives towards sustainability goals.

- **Prioritize Sustainable Shopping:** Make sustainable choices while shopping by choosing products with minimal packaging, choosing bulk items, and supporting brands committed to eco-friendly practices. Reduce your reliance on single-use packaging on grocery trips by bringing reusable bags, produce bags, and containers.

- **Invest in Reusable Alternatives:** Replace disposable items with their reusable counterparts. Switch to cloth napkins, stainless steel or glass containers, and durable, washable alternatives for items like straws or utensils. These replacements not only reduce waste but also contribute to long-term savings.

- **Compost Organic Waste:** Set up a composting system for organic waste, including kitchen scraps, yard trimmings, and certain paper products. Composting not only removes organic matter from landfills but also creates nutrient-rich compost that can enrich the soil and support plant growth.

- **Practice Mindful Food Management:** Minimize food waste by adopting conscious food management practices. Plan your meals, store food properly, and repurpose leftovers creatively. Composting or using food scraps for homemade broth are extra steps to ensure that every ingredient serves a purpose.

- **Repair and Upcycle**: Extend the lifespan of items by repairing them or repurposing them into new creations. Whether it's mending clothing, making, appliance repairs, or crafting DIY projects, embracing repairs and upcycling will make your home a hub of creativity.

- **Participate in Local Recycling Programs:** Familiarize yourself with local recycling programs and guidelines. Understand what materials are acceptable in your area and how to properly prepare them for recycling. Awareness of local recycling schemes ensures that household efforts are aligned with community waste management goals.

- **Reduce Energy Consumption:** Reduce energy consumption by adopting energy-efficient practices. From using LED lighting to investing in energy-efficient appliances, reducing your home's energy consumption contributes to overall resource conservation and aligns with waste reduction principles.

- **Educate and Involve Family Members:** Promote a sense of shared responsibility by educating and involving all family members in waste reduction efforts. Encourage open discussions about sustainability, brainstorm ideas together, and celebrate success as a collective. Creating a shared commitment to reducing household waste amplifies the impact of individual actions.

In conclusion, transforming our homes into sustainable havens involves making conscious choices in the fabric of our everyday lives. By adopting these household waste reduction tips, we are not only helping the environment but also embarking on a journey to become more responsible and mindful of our living spaces. As a sustainability expert, witnessing the integration of these practices into the home is like witnessing the creation of a sustainable home—a sanctuary where every choice resonates with the echoes of a green and harmonious future.

DIY and Repurposing Projects

Embarking on DIY and repurposing projects is a spirited journey into the realm of sustainability. It is an exploration where creativity intersects with conscious living. Let's explore the world of turning waste into wonders through practical initiatives that not only reduce our impact on the environment but also infuse creativity and ingenuity into our lives.

Upcycled Fashion: Unleash your creativity by upcycling clothing items. Turn old jeans into stylish tote bags, give new life to worn-out shirts with patches or embroidery, and discover the art of repurposing accessories. Upcycled fashion not only reduces textile waste but also allows for the expression of personal style through unique and sustainable creations.

Pallet Furniture: Embrace the art of pallet furniture creation to furnish your living spaces sustainably. Pallets, which are often thrown away after shipping, can be reused as coffee tables, bookshelves, or outdoor seating. This DIY project not only provides functional furniture but also showcases the beauty potential of reclaimed materials.

Mason Jar Marvels: Mason jars are a veritable gem in the world of DIY and repurposing. Use them as stylish storage containers, create ambient lanterns, or turn them into an herb garden. Mason Jar projects combine functionality with aesthetics, offering endless possibilities to reduce dependence on single-use containers.

Newspaper and Magazine Creations: Give new life to old newspapers and magazines through papier-mache projects. From decorative bowls and vases to intricate sculptures, papier-mache enables artistic expression while diverting paper waste from landfills. It's a tactile and visually appealing way to turn discarded learning materials into unique, long-lasting works of art.

Tire Planters and Swings: Discarded tires find new uses in DIY projects, such as vibrant planters or charming swings. The tire's flexibility and durability make it ideal for outdoor use. Repurposing tires not only keeps them out of landfills but also adds a touch of whimsy and greenery to our surroundings.

Wine Cork Creations: Keep wine corks and turn them into elegant creations. Craft a bulletin board, create unique coasters, or fashion a stylish trivet. Wine cork projects combine sophistication with sustainability, showcasing how a small, often overlooked item can become the focal point of functional art.

Repurposed Glass Bottles: Empty glass bottles make great lanterns or bright garden decorations in repurposing projects. By stringing lights through bottles or turning them into decorative plant holders, we extend the lifespan of the glass and add a warm, eco-friendly glow to your outdoor space.

Salvaged Wood Project: Discover the art of salvaged wood projects that will add beauty to your home. Old wooden pallets, discarded furniture, or scrap wood from construction sites can be repurposed into stylish shelves, photo frames, or even headboards. Salvaged wood projects not only reduce the need for new materials but also add character to your living space.

Plastic Bottle Greenhouses: Plastic bottles, often considered waste, can be turned into mini greenhouses for seedlings. By repurposing plastic bottles as a plant protection medium, DIY enthusiasts nurture sustainability from the start, promoting growth and keeping plastic out of the traditional waste stream.

Cloth Scrap Quilting: Turn fabric scraps into brightly colored quilts, blankets, or decorative tapestries. Not only does cloth scrap quilting give new life to discarded fabrics, but it also weaves a tapestry of resilience, preserving memories and creating functional and beautiful pieces for the home.

In conclusion, DIY and repurposing projects challenge us to rethink waste as a canvas for creativity and innovation. As a sustainability expert, witnessing discarded materials transformed into functional and aesthetic wonders is like observing a sustainable tapestry, one where every stitch and stroke tells the story of conscious living and the infinite possibilities that arise when we choose to shape our world with intention and ingenuity.

Chapter 8: Sustainable Gardening and Urban Farming

Cultivating an Eco-Friendly Garden

Embarking on the journey of cultivating an eco-friendly garden is a great endeavor - a celebration of biodiversity, sustainable practices, and the vibrant synergy between people and nature. As a sustainability specialist, let's explore the principles and

Sustainable Lifestyle Mastery

practices that transform gardens into a haven for ecological balance and mindful living.

- **Native Plant Selection:** Choose native plants suitable to the local climate, soil, and biodiversity. Native species support native pollinators, birds, and insects, promoting a resilient and balanced ecosystem. By adapting our gardens to the natural flora of the region, we contribute to the preservation of indigenous biodiversity.

- **Water-Wise Gardening:** Adopt water-conscious gardening practices to reduce water use. Use rain barrels to collect rainwater, incorporate drip irrigation systems, and mulch around plants to conserve soil moisture. Water-wise gardening not only conserves a precious resource but also improves plant health through conscious hydration.

- **Composting:** Composting kitchen waste, garden waste, and other organic materials creates a closed-loop system. Compost enriches soil with essential nutrients, improves water retention, and promotes a healthy microbial ecosystem. The art of composting reflects the cyclical nature of sustainable gardening, transforming waste into a valuable resource.

- **Natural Pest Control:** Maintain the delicate balance in the garden by using natural pest control methods. Encourage the reproduction of predatory insects, such as ladybugs and spiders, and encourage the growth of companion crops that protect against pests. By reducing reliance on synthetic pesticides, organic gardens become a haven for beneficial insects and biodiversity.

- **Sustainable Mulching:** Mulching not only suppresses weeds and conserves soil moisture, it also contributes to soil health. Use organic mulches such as wood chips, straw, or compost to create a protective layer that creates optimal conditions for plant growth. Sustainable mulching acts as a nurturing blanket for the garden ecosystem.

- **Integrated Pest Management (IPM):** Implement an integrated pest management (IPM) strategy that prioritizes a holistic, environmentally sensitive approach to pest control. By combining biological, cultural, and mechanical methods, eco-friendly gardens can effectively manage pests with minimal impact on non-target organisms and the overall ecosystem.

- **Biodiversity Boost:** Design gardens that attract a variety of wildlife, from bees and butterflies to beneficial birds and insects. Planting a variety of flowers, shrubs, and trees provides food and habitat, turning your garden into a vibrant ecosystem. Biodiversity not only enhances the visual appeal but also contributes to the ecological resilience of the space.

- **Eco-friendly Garden Design:** Craft a garden design that follows sustainable principles, balancing aesthetics with functionality. Incorporate edible plants, create rain gardens to manage runoff, and use vertical gardening to optimize your space. Eco-friendly garden design transforms outdoor spaces into living canvases of beauty and purpose.

- **Zero-Waste Harvesting:** Practice zero-waste harvesting by utilizing every part of the plants you grow. Explore creative ways to repurpose plant materials, from leaves and stems to fruit peels. Composting or making nutritious teas from plant residues completes the process, minimizing waste and maximizing ecological benefits.

- **Educational Outreach:** Extend the impact of your eco-friendly garden by sharing knowledge and inspiration with the community. Host workshops, create educational signage, or start a community garden project. By sowing seeds of sustainability, your garden becomes a catalyst for positive environmental change that transcends borders.

Simply put, cultivating an eco-friendly garden is a journey of stewardship—a dance in harmony with the natural world that celebrates the interconnectedness of all living things. Witnessing the transformation of outdoor spaces into sanctuaries of ecological balance and conscious living is like observing a garden of sustainable abundance. This is a testament to the profound impact that conscious cultivation has on the environment and future generations.

Urban Farming Practices

Embarking on the journey of urban farming is a transformative endeavor, one that challenges the constraints of space and brings life to the heart of vibrant urban landscapes. As a sustainability specialist, let's define urban farming and explore innovative and conscious practices that transform urban spaces into thriving centers of food production, community engagement, and ecological resilience.

1. **Vertical Gardening:** Vertical gardening is a symbol of ingenuity in the realm of urban farming. This practice uses vertical space on walls, balconies, or roofs to allow urban farmers to grow a variety of crops. Vertical gardens not only optimize space but also infuse urban environments with lush greenery, creating pockets of biodiversity within the concrete tapestry.

2. **Rooftop Farming:** The transformation of rooftops into agricultural landscapes is a hallmark of urban agricultural practices. Rooftop farms use underutilized space to grow crops, promoting local food production while providing respite from the effects of the urban heat island. These elevated oases not only contribute to food security but also serve as living laboratories for sustainable agriculture.

3. **Container Gardening:** Container gardening allows urban farmers to grow plants in a portable and versatile way. Whether using pots, barrels, or innovative containers, this method makes it easy to plant on balconies, patios, and even windowsills. Container gardening transforms small spaces into productive plots, allowing city dwellers to experience the joys of homegrown produce.

4. **Aquaponics:** In the dynamic realm of urban farming, aquaponics introduces a harmonious union of aquaculture and hydroponics. Fish and plants engage in a symbiotic relationship where nutrient-rich water from fish tanks feeds and nourishes plants, and the plants, in turn, filter and purify the water for the fish. This closed-loop system is an example of efficient use of resources in urban food production.

5. **Community Gardens:** Community gardens embody the spirit of cooperation and shared responsibility. These community spaces transform empty or neglected spaces into vibrant green spaces and promote a sense of belonging and food sovereignty. Urban farmers come together not only to grow crops but also to develop a shared commitment to sustainable living.

6. **Microgreens Cultivation:** Microgreens, the tender shoots of young plants, grow well in compact spaces and boast excellent nutrient density. Urban farmers are embracing microgreen cultivation as a way to produce nutritious greens in a short period of time. These small powerhouses contribute to local food systems and offer a fresh and delicious addition to urban diets.

7. **Permaculture Design:** Permaculture principles guide urban farming practices and mimic the wisdom of nature. By designing systems that maximize resource efficiency, reduce waste, and promote biodiversity, urban farmers create resilient and self-sustaining ecosystems within the confines of urban life. Permaculture design promotes urban oases that thrive in harmony with the natural world.

8. **Smart Agriculture Technologies:** Embrace smart farming technologies to optimize your urban farming activities. Automated irrigation systems, sensor-based monitoring, and precision agriculture technologies enable urban farmers to efficiently manage resources and meet the unique challenges of growing crops in urban environments.

9. **Edible Landscaping:** Through edible landscaping, urban farmers seamlessly weave edible elements into urban landscapes. Fruit trees, berry bushes, and herbs become integral parts of public spaces, parks, and residential areas. Edible landscaping not only improves the aesthetic appeal of urban areas but also fosters a connection between city dwellers and the food they consume.

10. **Agroforestry in Urban Spaces:** Agroforestry practices bring the benefits of trees to urban farming landscapes. Intercropping edible plants with fruit and nut trees improves biodiversity, provides shade, and supports soil health. The integration of agroforestry principles into urban spaces is an example of a holistic approach to sustainable food production.

In conclusion, urban farming practices seeds of change, sown amidst the concrete jungles of urban life. As a sustainability expert, witnessing the transformation of urban spaces into vibrant centers of food production and ecological resilience is akin to witnessing the evolution of cities. That is, a city where every rooftop, balcony, and communal garden blurs the lines between rural and urban to become a testament to the enduring spirit of sustainable living. Urban farms not only cultivate crops; they cultivate a vision of cities that thrive in harmony with nature, a vision that promises a future where abundance, community, and sustainability converge at the heart of the urban landscape.

Composting for a Greener Garden

Embarking on the journey of composting is an innovative step towards sustainable gardening. This is a practice that not only reduces waste but also enriches the soil with life-giving nutrients. As a sustainability expert, let's explore the art and science of composting and how this ancient practice can be the basis for creating a greener garden and promoting ecological balance.

The Alchemy of Composting: Composting is a magical process that transforms kitchen scraps, yard waste, and organic materials. Microorganisms, fungi, and bacteria work together in a symphony of decomposition to transform seemingly ordinary materials into nutrient-rich humus, also known as "black gold.". This alchemical process not only reduces landfill-bound waste but also creates a powerful elixir for soil health.

Building the Perfect Compost Pile: Creating the perfect compost pile requires a delicate balance of green and brown materials. Green materials, such as kitchen scraps and fresh plant material,   provide nitrogen, while brown materials, such as dry leaves and straw, supply carbon. Achieving the correct ratio provides an optimal environment for microorganisms to efficiently break down organic matter.

Kitchen Scraps: Kitchen scraps give life to compost piles. Fruit and vegetable peels, coffee grounds, and eggshells provide essential nutrients for compost. However, it is important to avoid adding meat, dairy, or fatty foods, as these can attract pests and interfere with the composting process.

Yard Waste: Fallen leaves, grass clippings, and pruned branches from the garden contribute valuable carbon to the compost mix. For faster decomposition, larger materials are shredded or chopped. Adding a variety of garden waste ensures a different nutrient profile in the final compost.

Compost Bin Selection: Choosing the right composting system depends on available space and personal preference. Compost bins, tumblers, and open-air piles each have their advantages. While bins and containers provide a controlled environment, open-air piles embrace a more natural and free-forming approach. The method you choose should suit your individual gardening needs and lifestyle.

Aeration and Turning: Oxygen plays an important role in the composting process. Turning the compost pile regularly or using an aeration system will promote airflow and prevent anaerobic conditions that can cause unpleasant odors. Adequate aeration speeds up decomposition and ensures a healthier and more productive compost.

Worm Composting: Worm composting, or vermicomposting, introduces red wigglers to the composting equation. These voracious eaters efficiently break down organic matter, producing nutrient-rich worm castings. Vermicomposting is a space-efficient, odor-free option that is ideal for indoor and outdoor composting.

Compost Tea: Compost tea, a nutrient-rich liquid extracted from compost, acts as a powerful elixir for plant health. By steeping compost in water, gardeners create a liquid fertilizer that improves soil structure, stimulates microbial activity, and promotes active plant growth. Compost tea is a sustainable solution for strengthening your garden ecosystem.

Troubleshooting Common Composting Challenges: Dealing with potential problems such as foul odors, pests, or slow decomposition is part of the composting process. By understanding common issues, gardeners can make reasonable adjustments to ensure a smooth and efficient composting process.

Closing the Loop: The culmination of the composting process is the application of finished compost to the garden. This nutrient-rich humus improves soil fertility, improves water retention, and promotes the activity of beneficial microorganisms. By returning compost to the soil, gardeners close the loop, contributing to a cycle of sustainability that makes gardens greener and the planet healthier.

In conclusion, composting goes beyond a gardening task to become a conscious and impactful act of stewardship. As a sustainability expert, witnessing kitchen and garden scraps transformed into nourishing elixirs for the soil is like witnessing a garden awakening to its full potential. Composting isn't just about reducing waste; it's about cultivating a cycle of regeneration that promotes a harmonious relationship between humanity and the Earth. Through composting, gardens become vibrant sanctuaries of life that embrace the transformative power of sustainable practices and promote a greener, more resilient planet.

Chapter 9: Building Sustainable Communities

Local Initiatives for Sustainable Living

Embarking on the journey of local initiatives for sustainable living is a collective endeavor, a shared commitment to promote resilience, ecological harmony, and community well-being. As a sustainability expert, let's take a look at the inspiring tapestry of initiatives that communities weave to build a sustainable, interconnected future.

Community Gardens: Community gardens are a testament to shared action and shared responsibility. These cultivated spaces not only yield fresh local produce but also become centers of knowledge exchange, fostering a sense of community pride and connection. As neighbors till the soil together, they cultivate not just crops but a shared vision for sustainable living.

Farmers Market: Farmers markets serve as bustling arenas where local farmers offer their harvests directly to the community. By supporting these markets, residents embrace the concept of "eating local" while reducing the carbon emissions associated with transporting food over long distances. The lively interactions at farmers' markets

Sustainable Lifestyle Mastery

become a celebration of local agriculture and sustainable food systems.

Renewable Energy Co-ops: Renewable energy cooperatives empower communities to harness clean energy collectively. From solar arrays to wind turbines, these cooperative efforts enable residents to invest in and benefit from renewable energy projects. Local sustainable energy initiatives not only reduce dependence on fossil fuels but also nurture energy resilience within communities.

Zero-Waste Community: The Zero Waste initiative redefines the concept of waste by encouraging conscious consumption, recycling, and composting. Local communities adopt practices that minimize landfill-bound materials, embracing a circular economy where resources are repurposed and recycled. Through these initiatives, communities turn waste into opportunities for sustainability and resource conservation.

Bike-Friendly Towns: Bike-friendly initiatives prioritize active and sustainable transportation options. Communities invest in bike lanes, cycling infrastructure, and bike-sharing programs to reduce dependence on cars. By encouraging cycling as a mode of transport, these initiatives will help promote healthy lifestyles, reduce traffic congestion, and reduce carbon emissions.

Green Building Programs: Green building initiatives focus on constructing and renovating buildings with environmentally friendly practices. From energy-efficient design to the use of sustainable materials, these programs promote eco-friendly structures that minimize their impact on the environment. Local communities promote green building as a pathway to creating resilient and energy-efficient neighborhoods.

Local Food Networks: Local food networks create direct connections between local farmers, producers, and consumers. Through Community-Supported Agriculture (CSA) models and farm-to-table programs, residents gain access to fresh, seasonal produce while supporting local agriculture. These networks enhance food security, promote biodiversity, and strengthen community ties.

Water Conservation Campaign: Communities are launching water conservation campaigns to protect this precious resource. Initiatives include educational programs to raise awareness about rainwater harvesting, efficient water management, and responsible water use. Local water conservation efforts contribute to the sustainable management of community water resources.

Eco-Friendly Transportation Hubs: Communities establish eco-friendly transportation hubs that prioritize sustainable transportation. Electric vehicle charging stations, bike-sharing programs, and efficient public transport options become key parts of these initiatives. By encouraging greener travel, communities can reduce carbon emissions and improve overall environmental sustainability.

Educational Outreach: Educational programs play an important role in nurturing sustainability knowledge in communities. Workshops, seminars, and community events provide residents with the knowledge and skills to make informed and sustainable choices. These initiatives promote a common understanding of environmental protection, helping people contribute to a more sustainable future.

In conclusion, local initiatives for sustainable living illuminate the transformative power of communities. As a sustainability specialist, seeing the mosaic of community-generated initiatives is like observing a garden blooming harmoniously. Local actions ripple outward, creating a resilient ecosystem for sustainable living. Through collaborative efforts, communities emerge as catalysts for change, sowing the seeds of a future where sustainability is not just a goal but an integral part of the collective ethos—a vision of interconnected, thriving localities contributing to a more sustainable and harmonious world.

Creating Eco-Conscious Neighborhoods

Embarking on the journey to create eco-conscious neighborhoods is a visionary endeavor, one that transcends infrastructure to weave a tapestry of sustainable living, community resilience, and ecological harmony. As your sustainability expert, let's take a look at the essential elements that transform neighborhoods into havens of eco-conscious living.

- ***Green Infrastructure:*** Green infrastructure is essential in eco-conscious neighborhoods. The integration of parks, green spaces, and urban forests not only increases the aesthetic appeal but also serves as an important lung for the community. Trees, plants, and natural habitats become essential components, promoting biodiversity and mitigating the urban heat island effect.

- **Sustainable Housing Design:** Eco-conscious neighborhoods prioritize sustainable home design that minimizes environmental impact. From energy-efficient homes to the use of eco-friendly materials, these neighborhoods embrace green building practices. The goal is to create homes that harmonize with the environment, using renewable energy sources and incorporating innovative designs for optimal energy efficiency.

- **Community Gardens:** Community gardens thrive as communal hubs, fostering a connection between residents and the land. These cultivated spaces not only provide fresh produce but also foster a sense of collective responsibility. Residents actively participate in growing local food, ensuring food security, and creating a vibrant tapestry of interconnected gardens.

- **Waste Reduction Initiatives:** Eco-conscious neighborhoods implement waste reduction initiatives that redefine the concept of waste. Comprehensive recycling programs, composting facilities, and public education campaigns encourage residents to reduce waste and repurposed materials. The goal is to create a circular economy that conserves resources and reuses them in society.

- **Pedestrian-Friendly Infrastructure:** Designing pedestrian-friendly infrastructure makes neighborhoods more walkable. Eco-conscious communities prioritize sidewalks, bike lanes, and pedestrian-friendly areas to reduce dependence on cars. This not only promotes a healthy lifestyle, but also reduces carbon emissions and increases the significance of community interaction.

- **Renewable Energy Integration:** Eco-conscious neighborhoods embrace the integration of renewable energy and use local, clean energy sources. Solar panels, wind turbines, and energy-efficient technologies are becoming mainstream in these communities. The aim is to reduce dependence on fossil fuels, reduce carbon emissions, and create a resilient energy system within the neighborhood.

- **Water Conservation Measures:** Sustainable water practices are a priority in eco-conscious neighborhoods. Rainwater harvesting, efficient irrigation systems, and water-saving technologies contribute to water conservation efforts. Residents are actively involved in initiatives to reduce water consumption and conserve this precious resource for current and future generations.

- **Local Food Networks**: Local food networks thrive in eco-conscious neighborhoods, creating direct links between farmers, producers, and residents. Farmers markets, Community Supported Agriculture (CSA) programs, and farm-to-table initiatives are becoming an integral part of the fabric of these communities. By supporting local agriculture, residents contribute to sustainable food systems and reduce the environmental impact of food transport.

- **Educational Outreach Programs**: Environmentally conscious neighborhoods prioritize sustainability literacy through educational programs. Workshops, seminars, and community events provide residents with the knowledge and skills to make informed and sustainable choices. These initiatives enable people to actively contribute to sustainable communities and develop a shared understanding of environmental protection.

- **Collaborative Governance:** Eco-conscious neighborhoods embrace collaborative governance models that empower residents as stewards of their environment. Residents actively participate in decision-making processes, contributing to the shaping of their community's sustainability goals. This collaborative approach fosters a sense of ownership and responsibility, ensuring the continued success of environmentally conscious initiatives.

In conclusion, the journey to create an eco-conscious neighborhood goes beyond the physical structures. It represents our collective commitment to a sustainable and harmonious lifestyle. As a sustainability professional, witnessing communities transform into beacons of sustainability is like witnessing an ecosystem flourish. Through collaborative efforts, eco-conscious neighborhoods emerge as models of resilience, interconnected living, and the potential to create homes in harmony with nature. Neighborhoods like these are living proof that when communities come together around a shared vision, they can build a sustainable and prosperous future, one neighborhood at a time.

Engaging in Community Sustainability Projects

Participation in sustainable community projects is a powerful catalyst for change. It is an opportunity for individuals to come together, pool resources, and weave together a tapestry of resilience, environmental stewardship, and lasting impact. As your sustainability specialist, let's explore the transformative potential of engaging in community sustainability projects and how these initiatives can shape a greener future.

Collaborative Visioning: Community sustainability projects often begin with a shared visioning session where residents come together to identify shared goals and aspirations. This collective process forms the basis for creating a sustainable blueprint that reflects the values, needs, and aspirations of the community.

Green Spaces and Urban Gardens: One of the hallmark projects embraced by communities is the creation of green spaces and urban gardens. Transforming vacant lots into vibrant, biodiversity-rich havens not only improves the aesthetic appeal of the neighborhood but also contributes to local food production, biodiversity, and community well-being.

Renewable Energy Installations: Communities participate in renewable energy projects such as installing solar panels or wind turbines, to harness clean and sustainable energy. These initiatives not only reduce our dependence on fossil fuels but also contribute to local energy resilience. Residents often have the opportunity to collectively invest in and benefit from these renewable energy sources.

Waste Reduction Campaigns: Waste reduction campaigns aim to transform the community's approach to waste management. Through recycling programs, composting initiatives and educational campaigns, residents actively participate in reducing waste and repurposing materials. These projects promote a circular economy mindset that conserves and reuses resources within communities.

Sustainable Transport Initiatives: Communities are prioritizing sustainable transport plans to reduce carbon emissions and promote eco-friendly commuting. This includes developing bike lanes, improving public transport options, and encouraging the use of electric vehicles. Sustainable transportation projects improve community health, reduce traffic congestion and contribute to cleaner air.

Community-Supported Agriculture (CSA) Programs: CSA programs connect local farmers directly with community members, providing fresh, seasonal produce. Residents have the opportunity to support local agriculture, reduce carbon emissions associated with food transportation, and strengthen connections to their food sources.

Water Conservation Projects: Water conservation projects focus on the preservation and responsible management of water resources within the communities. Through rainwater harvesting, efficient irrigation systems and education campaigns, residents can reduce their water consumption and contribute to the sustainable management of this important resource.

Eco-Education and Skill-Building Workshops: Sustainable community projects often include training workshops and skill-building sessions. These initiatives provide residents with the knowledge and skills they need to make sustainable choices in their everyday lives. Topics may range from energy conservation to sustainable gardening practices.

Restoration and Conservation Efforts: By participating in restoration and conservation projects, communities can conserve and enhance natural habitats. Residents participate in activities such as tree planting, habitat restoration, and clean-up efforts to protect the local ecosystem and biodiversity.

Community Resilience Planning: Community resilience planning is about preparing for and adapting to environmental changes and challenges. Through collaborative efforts, communities develop strategies to address potential risks such as extreme weather events, rising sea levels, or other climate-related impacts. This proactive approach ensures that communities can overcome challenges and become stronger and more resilient.

In conclusion, participating in community sustainability projects is like igniting a beacon of hope. It is a collective effort that has the power to transform communities and create a greener and more resilient future. As a sustainability professional, seeing communities come together for the greater good is a testament to the transformative potential of shared vision and collective action. Through these projects, individuals become stewards of their environment, contributing to a lasting legacy that is passed down from generation to generation. Community-led sustainable development projects are beacons of hope and demonstrate the profound impact that collective action can have in shaping a sustainable and harmonious world.

Chapter 10: Mindfulness and Well-being in Sustainable Living

The Connection Between Mindfulness and Sustainability

In the area of sustainability, there is a deep connection between mindfulness and the pursuit of a harmonious and eco-conscious existence. As a sustainability specialist, it is important to explore the symbiotic relationship between mindfulness practices and sustainable living, recognizing how the principles of mindfulness can promote positive change at the individual and planetary levels.

- ☐ **Cultivating Awareness:** At its core, mindfulness involves developing a heightened awareness or deep presence in the current moment. This guiding principle aligns seamlessly with the essence of sustainability, encouraging people to become conscious stewards of the environment by fully participating in their choices and actions.

☐ **Mindful Consumption:** Conscious consumption is an important aspect of sustainable living. By applying mindfulness to everyday choices, individuals become acutely aware of the impact their purchases have on the environment. From food to clothing, mindful consumption leads to informed decisions that prioritize ethical and sustainable products, promoting a more responsible and eco-friendly lifestyle.

☐ **Gratitude for Nature's Bounty:** Mindfulness encourages gratitude for nature's blessings. By cultivating a deep environmental awareness, people are more likely to engage in sustainable practices that protect and preserve our planet. This gratitude becomes a driving force for conscious action and fosters a sense of connection with nature.

☐ **Mindful Waste Management:** Mindful waste management involves a conscious approach to reduce, reuse, and recycle. Through mindfulness, individuals become attuned to the consequences of waste, inspiring sustainable practices such as composting, minimalism, and conscious disposal. Mindfulness transforms waste management into a conscious act of environmental stewardship.

☐ **Sustainable Choices informed by Mindful Reflection:** Mindfulness encourages reflective decision-making. When individuals approach choices with conscious thought, they are more likely to choose sustainable alternatives. Whether choosing eco-friendly transportation, supporting local businesses, or adopting a plant-based diet, thoughtful reflection guides individuals to make choices consistent with environmental sustainability.

- ☐ **Mindful Energy Consumption:** Mindful energy consumption involves conscious efforts to reduce energy consumption and adopt renewable energy sources. Through mindfulness practices, people become aware of their energy habits and actively seek ways to minimize their impact on the environment. This may include energy-efficient technologies, conservation practices, and advocating for renewable energy initiatives.

- ☐ **Emotional Resilience in the Face of Environmental Challenges:** Mindfulness promotes emotional resilience, an important trait when dealing with environmental challenges.

By cultivating mindfulness, individuals develop their ability to cope with eco-anxiety and climate-related stressors. This emotional resilience becomes an important tool for engaging in sustained, impactful, and environmental action.

- [ ] **Mindful Community Engagement:** Mindfulness extends beyond personal practices to community engagement. Conscious communities collaborate to achieve sustainability goals, share resources, and collectively address environmental challenges. Mindfulness-based interconnectedness becomes the driving force behind community-based sustainability initiatives.

- [ ] **Mindful Advocacy:** Mindfulness encourages individuals to become conscious advocates for environmental issues. By fully engaging with the environmental issues facing the world, individuals are encouraged to voice their opinions, raise awareness, and join movements advocating for positive change. Mindful advocacy is a powerful force driving systemic change toward sustainability.

☐ **Mindful Education:** Mindfulness in education plays an important role in shaping future eco-stewards. By incorporating mindfulness practices into educational curricula, individuals gain a deeper understanding of their role in protecting the environment. Mindful education becomes a catalyst for fostering a new generation dedicated to sustainable living.

In conclusion, the synergy between mindfulness and sustainability is a profound journey of conscious living, a journey where the principles of mindfulness become a catalyst for harmony on Earth. As a sustainability professional, recognizing and fostering these connections can help people turn their awareness into positive and sustainable action. The mindful pursuit of an eco-conscious existence not only benefits individuals on a personal level but also collectively contributes to the broader vision of a harmonious and sustainable world. Mindfulness enables people to become active participants in the planet's well-being story, fostering a legacy of mindful living for future generations.

Sustainable Self-Care Practices

In the realm of sustainability, the concept of self-care goes beyond individual well-being to include practices that are consistent with the health of both the individual and the planet. As your sustainability expert, let's explore the principles of sustainable self-care—practices that not only encourage a thriving sense of well-being but also contribute to a greater ecosystem of ecological harmony.

- ***Mindful Consumption of Personal Care Products***: Sustainable self-care starts with conscious choices of personal care products. People help reduce their impact on the environment by choosing eco-friendly, cruelty-free, and sustainably sourced items. Carefully reading ingredient lists and choosing products with minimal packaging will ensure that your personal care routine is in line with environmental stewardship.

- ***DIY and Upcycle Beauty Routines***: Embracing a sustainable approach to beauty involves exploring do-it-yourself (DIY) and upcycled options. From making homemade face masks to repurposing storage containers, individuals can curate beauty routines that reduce reliance on single-use products and promote a connection to sustainable and resourceful practices.

- **Nature-Inspired Wellness Activities:** Incorporating nature-inspired wellness activities into personal care routines creates a synergy between personal wellness and environmental appreciation. Activities such as forest bathing, outdoor yoga, and nature walks not only strengthen mental and physical health but also create a deep connection with nature.

- ***Sustainable Wardrobe Choices***: Building a sustainable wardrobe is an essential part of self-care. By choosing high-quality, timeless, and ethically produced clothing, you can help reduce fast fashion's impact on the environment. Embracing minimalist wardrobe principles encourages conscious consumption and promotes a healthier relationship with personal style.

- **Eco-Friendly Beauty and Grooming Tools**: Sustainable self-care includes the tools we use. Choosing eco-friendly beauty and grooming products such as bamboo toothbrushes, reusable razors, and refillable containers can help reduce plastic waste. These choices align personal grooming practices with a commitment to sustainable living.

- *Mindful Nutrition for Personal and Environmental Health*: Nourishing the body through mindful nutrition supports personal health and has a broader impact on the planet. By choosing seasonal, locally grown, and plant-based foods, you can reduce the carbon footprint associated with food production and promote sustainable agricultural practices.

- **Green Spaces and Wellness Sanctuaries:** Incorporating green space into self-care routines turns wellness practices into acts of environmental appreciation. Integrating nature into self-care rituals by cultivating a home garden or spending time in community parks can help you connect more deeply with the Earth and improve your well-being.

- **Sustainable Sleep Hygiene:** Prioritizing sustainable sleep hygiene involves making eco-conscious choices when it comes to bedding, mattresses, and sleepwear. By choosing organic, ethically produced materials and supporting companies with transparent and sustainable practices, you can ensure that restful sleep aligns with environmental responsibility.

- **Mindful Waste Management in Self-Care:** Sustainable self-care extends to waste management practices. Mindful disposal of personal care products, recycling packaging, and embracing zero-waste alternatives contribute to reducing the environmental impact of self-care routines. Individuals can explore creative ways to repurpose or recycle items commonly associated with personal care.

- **Eco-Friendly Fitness and Well-Being Practices:** Choosing eco-friendly fitness practices, such as outdoor workouts or participation in social activities, combines sustainability with self-care routines. Avoiding single-use plastics during workouts, supporting eco-conscious fitness brands, and engaging in green initiatives contribute to a holistic approach to well-being.

In conclusion, sustainable self-care practices involve a holistic approach to health, one that simultaneously nourishes individuals and the planet. As a sustainability professional, supporting these practices can help people see self-care as a profound act of environmental stewardship. By aligning personal well-being with sustainable choices, individuals contribute to the larger narrative of global harmony, promoting a world where the pursuit of personal health is perfectly aligned with a commitment to the health of the planet. Sustainable self-care is a transformative journey, a path toward wellness that resonates not only with the tranquility of individual rituals but also with the thriving vitality of the interconnected ecosystem we call home.

Balancing Personal and Planetary Well-being

The synergy between personal well-being and the health of the planet is a delicate dance in the pursuit of a sustainable lifestyle. That is, an interplay where individuals try to find a balance between self-care and protecting the health of the planet. As your sustainability expert, let's explore the principles of balancing personal and planetary well-being and understand how these interrelated aspects form the basis of a harmonious existence.

1. **Mindful consumption:** Balancing personal and planetary well-being starts with conscious consumption. People are encouraged to make choices that contribute not only to their health

but also to the health of the planet. By choosing sustainably produced and eco-friendly products, individuals embark on a journey where personal satisfaction meets environmental protection.

2. **Holistic Nutrition:** The concept of balancing personal and planetary well-being extends to nutrition. Adopting a plant-based diet not only benefits your health but also reduces the environmental impact of food production. By making conscious choices in the kitchen, individuals contribute to a sustainable and nourishing relationship with themselves and the planet.

3. **Eco-Conscious Lifestyle Choices:** To find a balance between personal happiness and the health of the planet, we must adopt an environmentally

conscious lifestyle. From energy-efficient home practices to sustainable transformation choices, individuals can incorporate sustainability into their everyday lives. This holistic approach ensures that individual actions reflect a commitment to balanced coexistence with the Earth.

4. **Mindful Waste Management:** Waste management practices become an important point of contact between the well-being of individuals and the planet. Conscious waste reduction, recycling initiatives, and composting efforts not only minimize individual carbon emissions but also contribute to the broader mission of global sustainability.

5. **Nature Connection:** Balancing personal and planetary well-being goes hand in

hand with strengthening our connection to nature. Spending time outdoors, whether through hiking, gardening, or simply enjoying the natural scenery can improve your mental health and environmental awareness. This harmonious relationship encourages humans to be stewards of the Earth.

6. **Sustainable Mindset in Personal Development:** Infusing personal development with a sustainable mindset ensures that individuals can thrive in harmony with the planet. This may include adopting minimalism, embracing conscious consumerism, and developing skills that contribute positively to both personal growth and environmental stewardship.

7. **Mindful Travel Practices:** For those who love to explore, balancing personal

and planetary well-being extends to travel practices. Conscious travel means choosing eco-friendly accommodations, supporting local communities, and reducing the impact of your travels on the environment. This personal adventure will be a journey towards responsible stewardship of our planet's diverse landscapes.

8. **Green Spaces as Sanctuaries for Well-Being:** The integration of green spaces into urban planning is becoming an important part of balancing personal and planetary well-being. Accessible parks, community gardens, and urban green spaces foster a symbiotic relationship between personal well-being and environmental health, creating spaces where people can rejuvenate mentally and physically.

9. **Sustainable Self-Care Practices:** The practice of sustainable self-care is a fusion of personal and planetary well-being. By choosing eco-friendly beauty products, adopting minimalist grooming routines, and incorporating nature-inspired wellness activities, individuals embark on a journey that seamlessly blends self-care and environmental awareness.

10. **Advocacy and Community Engagement:** The balance of personal and planetary well-being is enhanced through advocacy and community engagement. Individuals are encouraged to join the movement, support initiatives, and engage in conversations that promote personal health and environmental sustainability. Collective action is a powerful force for positive change on a global scale.

In conclusion, the art of balancing the well-being of individuals and the planet is a symbiotic dance—a harmonious interaction in which individuals and the planet coexist in a state of mutual care. As a sustainability professional, advocating for this delicate balance can help people recognize the deep connection between their well-being and the health of the planet. By encouraging a conscious and holistic approach to life, individuals not only develop a sense of personal fulfillment but also actively contribute to the wonderful tapestry of global sustainability. Balancing personal and planetary well-being is a journey, a conscious pursuit that combines self-care and stewardship of the Earth to create a legacy of balanced living for future generations.

Conclusion: A Lifetime of Sustainable Mastery

Reflecting on Your Sustainable Journey

Embarking on sustainable travel is more than a destination; it's an ongoing exploration characterized by continuous learning, adaptation, and conscious choice. As a sustainability professional, guiding individuals through a reflective process allows them to assess the impact of their decisions, celebrate successes, and set intentions for the future. Let's look at how important it is to reflect on your sustainable journey-a compass that guides us on our way to living in harmony with the Earth.

Acknowledging Progress: Reflecting on your sustainability journey starts with acknowledging the progress you've made along the way. Celebrate milestones, from small victories like reducing plastic consumption to major achievements like adopting a plant-based diet. Recognizing these achievements creates a sense of accomplishment and motivates individuals to continue making positive choices.

Learning from Challenges: All journeys are full of challenges, and sustainable lifestyles are no exception. Reflecting on the problems you encounter can give you valuable insight into areas that need adjustments. Whether it's overcoming compost barriers or facing sustainable shopping challenges, every hurdle is an opportunity for growth and improvement.

Assessing Ecological Footprint: An important aspect of reflection is assessing one's ecological footprint. Individuals can explore tools and calculators to quantify the environmental impact of their choices. This process focuses on areas where improvement is possible and guides people to make more informed and sustainable decisions in their daily lives.

Revisiting Intentions: Sustainable living is deeply rooted in personal values and intentions. Reflecting on the initial motivations for adopting sustainability allows individuals to reassess whether their actions are consistent with these core values. This realignment ensures that sustainable choices remain authentic and connected to the deeper purpose of fostering a healthy relationship with the Earth.

Explore New Opportunities: The journey towards sustainability is dynamic, and new opportunities for eco-friendly practices are constantly emerging. Thinking about your sustainable journey involves being open to innovation. Whether it's researching advancements in renewable energy, participating in community initiatives, or adopting new sustainable technologies, individuals can continue to improve their eco-conscious efforts.

Engaging in Community: Sustainability is often strengthened through community involvement. Reflecting on the collaborative aspect of the journey involves thinking about the impact that individual choices have on the wider community. Sharing experiences, insights, and challenges with like-minded individuals creates a network of support and inspiration, fostering a sense of collective responsibility for the planet.

Adapting to Changing Circumstances: As life evolves, so should one's sustainable practices. Reflecting on the journey also includes acknowledging the need for adaptation. Changes in your lifestyle, location, or personal circumstances may require adjustments to sustainable routines. This flexibility ensures that stability remains a dynamic and achievable endeavor despite life's changes.

Incorporating Mindfulness: Mindfulness plays a key role in living a sustainable life. Thinking about your sustainable journey involves being aware of your everyday choices. Conscious consideration of consumption, waste reduction, or energy consumption promotes a deeper connection with the environment and increases the overall impact of sustainable practices.

Setting Future Intentions: Reflection provides a basis for setting future intentions. Individuals can use their insights to create a roadmap for growth in their sustainable journey. Whether it's exploring new sustainable habits, participating in environmental initiatives, or advocating for positive change, setting intentions propels individuals forward on their path towards a more eco-conscious lifestyle.

Inspiring Others: Reflecting on your sustainability journey goes beyond personal growth and becomes an opportunity to inspire others. By sharing experiences, successes, and lessons learned, individuals can become catalysts for positive change in their communities. This ripple effect transforms individual efforts into a collective movement towards a more sustainable and harmonious world.

In conclusion, reflecting on your sustainable journey is a powerful tool for continued growth and positive change. As a sustainability specialist, encouraging individuals to continuously assess their impact, celebrate their achievements, and set goals will make their journey towards sustainability vibrant and dynamic. Through reflection, individuals not only deepen their relationship with the Earth but also contribute to the global movement towards a sustainable and harmonious life. It is an ongoing process that transforms individual actions into a collective effort to positively change the environment.

Inspiring Others to Join the Movement

As a sustainability specialist, one of the most rewarding aspects of the journey is the opportunity to inspire others to embrace a lifestyle that nourishes both individuals and the planet. The movement towards sustainability is based on collective action, and your role will be essential in accelerating global change. Let's explore the strategies and insights that can effectively inspire others to join this transformative movement toward a more sustainable and harmonious world.

- **Lead by Example:** The most effective way to inspire others is to lead by example. Demonstrate the authenticity of a sustainable lifestyle through conscious consumption choices, waste reduction, and green practices. Your experience becomes tangible and relatable evidence of the positive impact of sustainable living.

- **Share Personal Journey:** Harness the power of storytelling to create meaningful connections. Share your journey towards sustainability-highlight challenges, triumphs, and the profound changes experienced. Storytelling goes beyond facts and figures to evoke emotions that resonate more deeply with individuals, making sustainable living more accessible and relatable.

- **Educate and Raise Awareness:** Inspiration often stems from understanding. Educate others about the impact their choices have on the environment and the benefits of sustainable living. Use accessible and engaging platforms, whether through workshops, online content, or community events, to raise awareness and empower individuals with the information needed to make informed decisions.

- **Showcase Positive Outcomes:** Illustrate the positive outcomes of sustainable living, both at the individual level and in contributing to global well-being. Showcase tangible results, whether it's reduced carbon emissions, healthier lifestyles, or the conservation of natural resources. Demonstrating the impact of our collective efforts increases our sense of purpose and motivation.

- **Collaborate with Communities:** Collaboration is at the heart of any innovative movement. Engage with local communities, environmental organizations, and like-minded people to build a network of support. By fostering a sense of belonging and shared purpose, we increase collective impact and create a supportive environment where individuals can embark on their sustainable journey.

- **Empowerment through Small Steps:** Recognize that not everyone may be ready to radically change their lifestyle. Inspire others by emphasizing the accessibility of sustainable living through small, achievable steps. Empowering individuals with manageable actions, whether it's reducing single-use plastic, growing a home garden, or adopting a meat-free Monday encourages gradual but impactful change.

- **Highlight Diverse Perspectives:** Make sure the sustainability movement is inclusive and embraces diverse perspectives. Present stories and experiences from diverse backgrounds, cultures, and communities. Celebrating diversity within a movement creates a space where people from all walks of life can be inspired and contribute in unique ways.

- **Encourage Collective Action:** Inspiration flourishes when individuals witness the impact of collective action. Encourage and participate in community activities such as cleanups, tree-planting campaigns, or sustainable living challenges. By demonstrating that change is a shared effort, you build a sense of shared responsibility and purpose.

- **Provides Practical Resources:** Provide practical resources to accelerate your journey to sustainability. Develop guides, toolkits, or online resources that offer actionable steps, tips, and information. By making sustainable living more accessible and less intimidating, individuals are encouraged to take the first steps towards a greener lifestyle.

- **Foster a Culture of Positivity:** Inspiration thrives in a culture of positivity. Celebrate the progress, no matter how small, and cultivate optimism. By focusing on the positive impact individuals can make, you create a stimulating environment that encourages sustained commitment to the sustainability movement.

In conclusion, inspiring others to join the movement towards sustainability is a special journey with great results. As a sustainability specialist, your influence contributes to a ripple effect of positive change beyond individual actions. By leading with authenticity, sharing stories, and developing a supportive community, you become a catalyst for a global transition to a more harmonious and sustainable world. Together, as a united force, we can create a future where the choices we make nurture both personal well-being and the health of our planet.

Appendix: Resources for Sustainable Living

Recommended Books, Documentaries, and Websites

As a sustainability expert, guiding individuals toward a more conscious and environmentally friendly lifestyle means providing invaluable resources that enlighten, inform, and inspire. Here, we'll look at a curated list of recommended books, documentaries, and websites that serve as an insightful guide on the journey to sustainable living. These resources are designed to instill a deeper understanding, nurture minds, and broaden perspectives on the interrelationship between personal choices and the well-being of the planet.

☐ **Books:**

1. *"Braiding Sweetgrass: Indigenous Wisdom, Scientific Knowledge, and the*

Teachings of Plants" by Robin Wall Kimmerer:

This fascinating exploration combines indigenous wisdom and scientific knowledge to provide an in-depth perspective on our relationship with nature and the importance of reciprocity.

2. *"Doughnut Economics: Seven Ways to Think Like a 21st Century Economist" by Keith Raworth:*

Kate Roworth challenges traditional economic thinking to embrace sustainability and social justice, proposing an innovative model that challenges readers to reimagine the future.

3. *The Uninhabitable Earth: Life After Warming" by David Wallace-Wells:*

Wallace-Wells presents a serious yet compelling story that explores the consequences of climate change and highlights the urgency of collective action.

4. **"Cradle to Cradle: Remaking the Way We Make Things" by William McDonough and Michael Braungart:** McDonough & Braungart present a visionary approach from design to disposal, advocating for products and systems that contribute positively to the environment.

☐ **Documentaries:**

1. **"Our Planet" (Netflix):** Narrated by Sir David Attenborough, this visually stunning series explores the beauty of nature while highlighting the pressing environmental challenges it faces.

2. **"True Cost" (2015):** This documentary examines the impact of the fashion industry on the environment and

workers, highlighting the importance of making ethical and sustainable fashion choices.

3. **"Before the Flood" (2016):** Leonardo DiCaprio takes viewers on a journey around the world to witness the impacts of climate change, offering insights into possible solutions and the need for urgent action.

4. **"A Plastic Ocean" (2016):** This documentary addresses the critical issue of plastic pollution in the oceans and encourages prompt reflection on individual consumption habits and the broader implications they have on marine ecosystems.

☐ **Websites:**

1. **Earth911:**
   (https://earth911.com/): Earth911 is a comprehensive resource for sustainable living, offering information on recycling, eco-friendly products, and tips for reducing environmental impact.

2. **The Story of Stuff:**
   (https://www.storyofstuff.org/): Founded by Annie Leonard, this platform explores the life cycle of consumer goods, encouraging conscious consumption and advocating for a more sustainable economy.

3. **Ecocult:** (https://ecocult.com/): Ecocult is an online destination for sustainable fashion and lifestyle, that provides

information on ethical brands, sustainable travel, and eco-friendly living.

4. **Climate Visuals:** (https://climatevisuals.org/): Climate Visuals is a unique resource focused on climate change communication, offering a library of images to convey climate-related issues more effectively.

In conclusion, these recommended books, documentaries, and websites serve as beacons of knowledge, guiding individuals towards a deeper understanding of sustainable living. As a sustainability expert, your role is not only to inform, but also to spark curiosity and inspire a sense of responsibility towards the planet. By exploring these resources, individuals can develop awareness and make informed choices that contribute to a more sustainable and harmonious future for all.

Sustainable Living Challenges and Communities

The journey to sustainable living is a laudable endeavor, but it is not without its share of challenges. As a sustainability specialist, it is important to address these barriers and, more importantly, foster resilient communities that can overcome them together. Let's look at some of the common challenges individuals face on their journey to sustainable living and the transformative power of communities in navigating and overcoming these obstacles.

Consumption Habits and Convenience Culture: One of the key challenges will be reshaping established consumer habits and the pervasive convenience culture. The ease of single-use items and fast consumption pose a considerable barrier. Sustainable communities play an important role in sharing alternatives, and experiences, and supporting each other in making informed choices.

Sustainable Access and Affordability: Limited access to sustainable products and affordability concerns may hinder progress. Sustainable living communities can act as information hubs, sharing cost-effective alternatives, DIY solutions, and advocating for more accessible eco-friendly options within local markets.

Greenwashing and Ethical Consumption: The prevalence of greenwashing (misleading claims made by companies about the environment) can lead to confusion. Sustainable living communities contribute by critically evaluating products, sharing information, and creating a collective demand for transparency and authenticity in eco-friendly branding.

Recycling Challenges and Waste Reduction: Despite recycling efforts, waste management problems persist. Sustainable communities provide platforms for members to share practical tips on waste reduction, managing recycling systems, and providing collective support for improving waste management infrastructure.

Limited Sustainable Infrastructure: In some regions, development is hampered by a lack of sustainable infrastructure. Sustainable living communities can influence change by working with local authorities, supporting eco-friendly policies, and promoting initiatives that enhance the overall sustainability of their communities.

Social Pressures and Lifestyle Expectations: Individuals often face social pressure and societal expectations that may conflict with sustainable choices. Communities create a supportive environment where members can share strategies for navigating social situations, advocating for sustainable practices, and promoting understanding within their circles.

Information Overload and Green Fatigue: The sheer volume of information about sustainable living can be overwhelming, leading to eco-fatigue. Communities streamline information, distilling it into practical guides, success stories, and interactive discussions to make the sustainable living journey more accessible and sustainable over the long term.

Balancing Individual and Collective Impact: While individual actions can make a difference, there's a need for collective impact to drive systemic change. Sustainable communities serve as platforms for collaboration, enabling members to amplify their impact through joint initiatives, community projects, and joint advocacy.

Navigating Climate Anxiety: The urgency of climate issues can trigger anxiety and feelings of helplessness. Sustainable communities provide emotional support, encourage open dialogue about climate anxiety, and create a sense of collective empowerment in the face of global challenges.

Overcoming Resistance to Change: Resistance to change, whether personal or societal, is a common barrier. Sustainable communities create space for shared stories of change and demonstrate that small, incremental changes can collectively have a significant positive impact.

In conclusion, sustainable living challenges require a collective and community-based approach. Sustainable living communities act as catalysts for change, providing support, resources, and a shared vision to help individuals overcome obstacles in their sustainable journey. As a sustainability specialist, fostering these communities is not only about mitigating challenges but also about building resilient networks that bring about positive change and create a more sustainable and harmonious future for all.

Index

A Comprehensive Index for Quick Reference Throughout the Book.

Having a trusted guide is essential to getting started on the path to sustainable living. This comprehensive index serves as a compass to easily navigate the book's diverse and enlightening content. Think of it as a road map that will guide you through the multifaceted landscape of sustainable living, support you in making informed choices, and help you gain a deeper understanding of the interrelationship between your actions and the well-being of our planet.

A - Authentic Living:

It explores the meaning of authenticity in sustainable living, emphasizing the profound impact of realistic and conscious choices.

B - Circular Economy:
Learn about the principles of the circular economy, which aims to reduce waste and increase resource efficiency.

C - Community Engagement:
Explores the role of communities in sustainable living, emphasizing the power of collective action and shared values.

D - Eco-friendly practices:
This comprehensive section highlights environmental practices that can be implemented in everyday life, from waste reduction to energy-saving habits.

E - Ethical Consumerism:
Unraveling the complexities of ethical consumerism will help readers make informed choices that align with their values.

F - Food Sustainability:

Explore a sustainable food landscape, including discussions about plant-based diets, local sourcing, and reducing food waste.

G - Green Technologies:

From renewable energy to eco-friendly innovations, we highlight innovative green technologies that promote sustainable living.

H - Holistic Wellness:

Exploring the intersection of sustainability and personal well-being, highlighting the symbiotic relationship between the two.

I - Informed Choices:

Empowering readers with information on how to critically evaluate and make informed choices in their sustainable journey.

J - Journey Reflections:

A section dedicated to personal development, overcoming challenges, and the evolving journey towards a sustainable life.

K - Kids and Sustainability:

It addresses the importance of instilling sustainable values in the younger generation and increasing environmental awareness from an early age.

L - Local initiatives:

Showcasing grassroots movements and local initiatives that contribute to community sustainability and environmental conservation.

M - Mindful consumption:

Encouraging a mindful approach to consumption, emphasizing quality over quantity, and making informed decisions.

N - Nature Connection

Emphasizing the deep connection between individuals and nature and exploring the benefits of nature immersion and conservation efforts.

O - Ocean Conservation:

Highlighting the critical importance of ocean conservation, addressing issues like plastic pollution, and advocating for the health of marine ecosystems.

P - Permaculture Practices:

Learn the principles of permaculture, an innovative approach to sustainable agriculture and land use.

Q - Questions for Reflection:

Provides thought-provoking questions to encourage self-reflection and contemplation throughout the journey to sustainable living.

R - Responsible Travel:

Sustainable Lifestyle Mastery

Explore sustainable and responsible travel practices with a focus on cultural sensitivity, environmental preservation, and community engagement.

S - Sustainable Fashion:
Explore the world of sustainable fashion with a focus on ethical practices, conscious consumerism, and eco-friendly alternatives.

T - Technology and Sustainability:
From green innovations to digital tools for eco-conscious living, we explore the role of technology in promoting sustainability.

U - Urban Sustainability:
Explores challenges and solutions for sustainable urban living, including eco-friendly infrastructure and community initiatives.

V - Vegan Living:

Discuss the principles and benefits of a vegan lifestyle, highlighting the positive impact a plant-based diet has on the environment.

W - Water Conservation:

Emphasize the importance of water conservation with tips on how to reduce water use and conserve the precious resource.

X - (e)Xploring New Horizons:

Encouraging readers to explore new horizons, embrace innovative ideas, and continuously evolve in their practice of sustainable living.

Y - Youth Engagement:

Focusing on the engagement of the youth in sustainable initiatives, acknowledging their role as catalysts for change.

Z - Zero Waste Living:

Sustainable Lifestyle Mastery

Unpacking the principles of zero waste living, providing practical tips and information on reducing waste, and adopting a circular lifestyle.

In conclusion, this comprehensive index serves as a comprehensive tool for sustainable living exploration. Whether you're looking for information on ethical consumerism, tips for reducing your carbon footprint, or reflections on your travel, this index is designed to provide smooth navigation to help you get the most out of the book's valuable content. Let the Sustainable Living Compass be your guide as you embark on a journey of transformation to a more conscious and harmonious lifestyle.